Holy

SPIRIT

The Promise
Left for the Believer

Holy
SPIRIT

The Promise
Left for the Believer

DEBORAH G. HUNTER

Hunter Heart Publishing
Colorado Springs, Colorado

Holy Spirit: The Promise Left for the Believer
Copyright © 2016 by Deborah G. Hunter
First Edition: May 2016

All definitions used in this book are taken from the Merriam-Webster online dictionary. All Hebrew/Greek definitions taken from Strong's Exhaustive Concordance of the Bible with Dictionaries of the Hebrew and Greek Words.

To order products, or for any other correspondence:

Hunter Heart Publishing
4164 Austin Bluffs Parkway, Suite 214
Colorado Springs, Colorado 80918
www.hunterheartpublishing.com
Tel. (253) 906-2160 – Fax: (719) 528-6359
E-mail: publisher@hunterheartpublishing.com
Or reach us on the internet: www.hunterheartpublishing.com
"Offering God's Heart to a Dying World"

This book and all other Hunter Heart Publishing™, Eagles Wings Press™ and Hunter Heart Kids™ books are available at Christian bookstores and distributors worldwide.

Chief Editor: Gord Dormer
Book cover design: Phil Coles Independent Design
Layout & logos: Exousia Marketing Group www.exousiamg.com
ISBN: 978-1-937741-51-8
Printed in the United States of America.

Dedication

I dedicate this book to the One who speaks to and through my spirit. The One who invades the earth realm and relays God's divine purposes & appointments for mankind; the One who is the Comforter, the Instructor, the Helper, the Teacher, the Gift, the One who raised Jesus from the dead, the One who is the Promise left for us here in this earth...

...Holy Spirit.

~May you learn to hear His voice and be led by Him.~

Acknowledgments

I want to acknowledge some of the pioneers who have spoken as the voice of God in this earth. I thank God for their obedience, their humility, their love for humanity and their boldness in Christ. It is *evident* Holy Spirit's working in their lives and ministries for the glory of Father God.

Katherine Kuhlman
A.W. Tozer
T.L. Osborn
John G. Lake
Reinhard Bonnke
Dr. Martin Luther King, Jr.
Billy Graham

William Seymour
Leonard Ravenhill
Charles Spurgeon
Mother Teresa
D.L. Moody
Smith Wigglesworth
Dr. Myles Monroe

I also want to acknowledge some very important people that God has allowed to encourage, exhort, empower, and equip me in following the voice of Holy Spirit over the years:

Pastor Donald Watkins
Apostle Steven W. Banks
Dr. Dennis Sempebwa
Pastora Mariet Perez
Dr. Will Moreland
Hilary Amara
LaShorne Zarlengo

Foreword

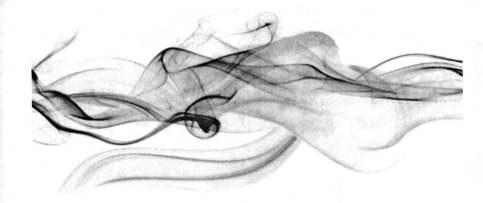

Holy Spirit is thoroughly researched from a historical, as well as biblical perspective; however, this book is useful and needed for much more than a theological reference. It reveals the explosive, yet personal interactive engagement of Holy Spirit with the Believer. As a member of the Godhead, His vibrant ministry is being executed in the earth realm through those who are sensitive and dependent upon Him from individuals, to people groups in remote distant lands, to the multitudes worshiping in overflowing stadiums throughout the earth. *Holy Spirit* will inform and will enable the reader to personally encounter this Person, this co-equal of the Godhead.

Regrettably, many human actions have been ascribed to Holy Spirit from a blasphemous perspective. This practice is aided by the fact that He remains largely unknown and misunderstood by many. We do a great disservice if our knowledge of Holy Spirit is limited to "shouting, dancing and tongues". *Holy Spirit* will aid in changing that view by dispelling misinformation and bringing readers to an informed and empowering revelation concerning His person and ministry. I encourage the readers not only to read this to strengthen their intellect and increase their knowledge, but as you delve into this masterful work by Deborah G. Hunter, prepare to embark upon new dimensions of your spiritual walk as a testament to this brilliant book, *Holy Spirit*.

Steven W. Banks
Apostle and Author

Table of Contents

Prologue

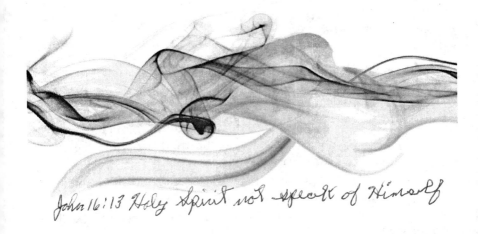

John 16:13 Holy Spirit not speak of Himself

From the inception of Creation, the Spirit of God, Holy Spirit, has been with us. In fact, He was before. The hovering existence of God in the sphere of space and time, Holy Spirit is fully God, operating within a realm that cannot contain the fullness of God the Father. The Spirit of God is creative; He enters and carries out the perfect will of God in the earth realm. Only seven times is Holy Spirit mentioned in the King James Version of the Bible; over one-hundred instances, He is revealed in the New Testament as Holy Spirit. In the original King James, He is seen as the "Holy Ghost" about eighty-nine times, but there is no mention in any other translation as "Holy Ghost". The word *ghost* was used in the King James Version in the year 1611 and was originally translated as meaning "an immaterial being". Most recently, the word "Spirit" replaced the word *ghost* in the Word of God mainly because words tend not to hold their meaning over the years. In the days of Shakespeare and King James, the word *ghost* meant the living essence of a person. The words "breath" and "soul" were synonymous with the word *ghost*. During those times, the word "spirit" was seen as the essence of a departed person or a demonic or paranormal apparition. As language evolved, people started saying *ghost* when speaking of the vision of a dead person, while "spirit" became the standard term for life or living essence, often referred to as the "soul." With slight exceptions, *ghost* and "spirit" changed places over some three hundred years.

To better see what these words meant before these translations, let's see what the Hebrew and Greek versions reveal to us. The word "Ghost" in the Greek translation is the word *hagios*, which means an awful thing; sacred, pure, blameless, religious, consecrated, holy, or saint. The word "Spirit" in the Greek translation is the word *pneuma* meaning a current of air, breath (blast), or a breeze; a spirit (human), the rational soul, vital principle, mental disposition, (superhuman), an angel, demon, or (divine) God, Christ's spirit, the Holy Spirit, ghost, life spirit (ual, ually), mind. Now let's look at the Hebrew translation of these words. The word "Ghost" is the word *gava*, which means to breathe out, expire, die, be dead, give up the ghost, or perish. The word "Spirit" is the word *ruwach* meaning wind, by resemblance of breath; sensible (or even violent exhalation); life, anger, insubstantiality, a region of the sky; by resemblance spirit, but only of a rational being (including its expressions and functions), air, anger, blast, breath, cool, courage, mind, quarter, side, spirit (ual), tempest, vain, (whirl) wind (y).

However each of these words is defined, both are intended to be used interchangeably as the Spirit of God Himself. Though we see Him on the scene very early on in the scriptures, many Christians, those who have believed, received and confessed Jesus Christ as their Lord and Savior, do not believe in, receive, or acknowledge Him. It is a very devastating reality. It is very encouraging to know people are turning their lives over to Jesus, and that they will have eternal life with the Father in Heaven, but the life they will lead here on earth without Holy Spirit is automatic denial, discouragement and defeat. God desires for us to live eternally with Him, but He also wants us to live, move and breathe in all power and authority here in this world. The Word of God in Genesis says we are to "be fruitful, multiply, fill the earth and subdue it and have dominion." (Genesis 1: 28) Without the access Holy Spirit provides, we are not able to carry out this scripture, let alone be true witnesses of Jesus in this earth.

Holy Spirit is necessary in our lives to carry the Gospel of Jesus Christ to the ends of the earth, and to effectively do all God has called us to do for Him. My prayer is, as you read this very thorough look into who Holy Spirit is, that you will, if you have not already, accept Him into your life and allow Him to do all He is called to do. His assignment is just as, if not more, important as yours. In fact, you will not be able to fulfill your assignment in this earth without Him. You do not have to be afraid of Him. He is not a ghost; He is not spooky. He has been sent! God gave us His only Son, Jesus Christ, to redeem us from the curse of Adam. And when Jesus fulfilled His earthly assignment, He, too, did not leave us without help. Before He ascended to be with the Father, He released and activated the ministry assignment of Holy Spirit in this earth. Join me on this journey and get to know Him intimately today!

Chapter 1
The Godhead

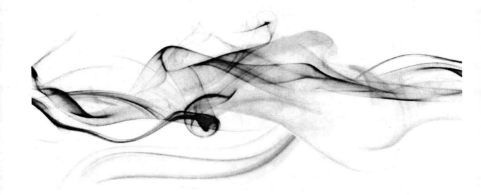

"Beware lest anyone cheat you through philosophy and empty deceit, according to the tradition of men, according to the basic principles of the world, and not according to Christ. For in Him dwells all the fullness of the Godhead bodily; and you are complete in Him, who is the head of all principality and power." Colossians 2:9

Throughout the history of Christianity, we have seen division of every sort, whether in denomination or doctrine. Each faction of Christianity holds a portion of Truth in its canon. In fact, every religion on the face of the earth holds some truth of the Word of God. Yet, not understanding, half-truths are no truth at all. The Scriptures say not to take away or add to any portion of the Word of God. But far too often, we desire to take what we want from scripture and deny the rest. Many believe in God, a higher power, or Creator of the Universe. Those who call themselves Christians believe in Jesus Christ as the Son of God. Other religions believe in Jesus as a prophet who did, indeed, perform miracles on the earth, and some believe that He died and rose from the dead, yet refuse to claim He is, in fact, the Son of the Living God.

From the Torah, to the Bible to the Qur'an, each has an account of Creation and each; fundamentally, carry a concept of the Godhead. The Torah, the Jewish canon, is, in essence, the first five books of the Christian Bible. The Torah is also known as the *Chumash, Pentateuch* or *Five Books of Moses*. The Torah is considered the "Law" of God. Many Jewish rabbis and theologians have given their thoughts and opinions on the spiritual inspiration of the Torah, written by Moses. Some believed it was inspired by God, while others believe it was merely a historical premise for the nation of Israel. Either way, they agree on the fact that Moses wrote the Torah, and that he was a prophet of God, implying that he had, indeed, been "inspired" to write the Words of God, the Law of God, for the Jewish people. The Spirit of the Living God, as revealed in both the Torah and the Bible, spoke to Moses through the 'Burning Bush' on Mount Sinai and delivered to him the Law, or the Ten Commandments. So, we are to conclude that as a "prophet," he heard the voice of God.

The Qur'an and it followers, Muslims, believe the Torah is divine and also believe that Moses was a prophet of God (Allah). They believe he received the Torah from God, which also implies an inspired, or supernatural, means of relaying it to Moses. The Torah and the Bible portray this account as the direct voice of God, speaking to Moses on Mount Sinai. The voice of God is likened to the Spirit of God, or *Holy Spirit*. The many contradictions highlighted in the Qur'an surely demolish any claims that the "revelation" given to their prophet, Muhammad, is not a corruption of, but reliably builds upon, Judeo-Christian history. Let's take a look at scripture from the Qur'an:

Qur'an, Sura 2:87--"We gave Moses the Book and followed him up with a succession of Apostles; We gave Jesus the son of Mary clear (signs) and strengthened him with the Holy Spirit."

This verse in Muslim religion reveals that not only do they believe the Torah was inspired by God (Allah) and given to Moses, but there is direct reference to Holy Spirit in their scriptures, as well as the Godhead.

Sura 4:171 "He received the *Spirit* as a helper so that he could raise the dead from the grave."

Muslims, in earlier times, recognized Jesus as being born by the Spirit of God (Allah), the spirit of Holy, and that He received (by whom, God) a helper, Holy Spirit, so He, Jesus, could raise the dead. This is the Godhead, revealed in Muslim scripture. Many other Muslims, including prominent figures, have also referenced this truth. Read the account of King Hassan II:

"At a synod in Casablanca, King Hassan II made a strong statement about Ayatollah Khomeini in Khomeini's last year of power: "If Khomeini will not stop his people from saying that he is the spirit of God or the spirit of the Holy he must be excluded from Islam and considered to be no longer a Muslim but a blasphemer, because there is only one in this world and the next who has the right to call himself the spirit of Allah. This is the son of Mary because he was born by the spirit of Allah.""[i]

King Hassan II was the King of Morocco from 1961 till his death in 1999. He was the 21st Monarch of the Alaouite Dynasty and had very close ties to Israel and the Jewish leaders. He understood the divinity of Jesus, as well as God the Father and Holy Spirit. Just as Muhammad and Ayatollah Khomeini, he was merely a man, born to both mother and father, not by the Spirit of God. What a testimony of reverence to Holy God and the close proximity that Islam has to the Torah and the Bible.

Let's look at several other scriptures in the Qur'an that point to Holy Spirit (emphasis added):

Sura 5:110: "[The Day] when Allah will say, "O Jesus, Son of Mary, remember My favor upon you and upon your mother when I supported you with the Pure *Spirit*...""

Sura 16:102: "Allah has sent the *Spirit of the Holy* from the Lord truly to strengthen those who believe."

Sura 17:85: "Allah told me that you will ask me about the *Spirit*. I have to say to you, the *Spirit* belongs to God, not to men, and you have only received a little knowledge about the *Spirit*."

Sura 21:91: "And we blew in her from our *spirit*, and we made her and her son both ayatollahs for all the worlds."

Sura 26:193-194: "We have sent down the faithful *Spirit* on your heart that you will be one who warns."

Sura 32:9: "After he had been formed, Allah blew in him from his *Spirit*."

Sura 38:72: "After I formed him, I blew in him from my *Spirit*."

Muslims, in thought, believed and still believe that the Spirit of Holy was the angel Gabriel. Muhammad tried, unsuccessfully, to explain Holy Spirit in his own limited knowledge. He knew scripture (Torah), as well as accounts from Believers, as he was born in 570 and most evidently heard the accounts of Jesus from His followers. In referencing Holy Spirit as the Spirit of Holy, Muhammad never had the revelation of Jesus Christ; neither have many of his followers since. Since there is no true acceptance of Holy Spirit in Islam, there is no knowledge of the Father and the Son and the Spirit, because the Spirit testifies that God is our Father and no one can call Jesus Christ Lord, except by Holy Spirit. The Muslim community has so much scripture at its disposal to know the Truth. Let us pray that Holy Spirit will touch them and open their eyes up to Jesus Christ as their Lord and Savior.

Now let us look to the Torah, the first five books of Moses, to see what the Jewish people believe of Holy Spirit. We know from the Beginning of Genesis: Father, Son and Holy Spirit were all together, as One, in Creation. The *Tanakh*, the Hebrew Scriptures, as well as many Talmudic and Rabbinical writings and teachings, reveal the triune concept of God (Elohim).

> "And (Elohim) said. Let us make man in our image, after our likeness: and let them have dominion over the fish of the sea, and over the fowl of the air, and over the cattle, and over all the earth." Genesis 1:26

God (Elohim) created man from a triune thought, according to Torah. Man was created body, soul and spirit, a triumvirate being, by "us". Who was God referring to in this passage of scripture? Just journey back a few scriptures to Genesis 1:1-2 where God the Father, God the Son and God the Holy Spirit were all in operation creating the world. This scripture is referenced in Torah and the Bible, as well as vaguely in the Qur'an. In studying other religions, I found similar references to vague ideas of a possible Holy Spirit in their teachings.

In Hinduism, there is what is called the *Purusha*, known as the indwelling witness Spirit. The *Purusha* is also known as the *kshetragna*, or knower of the body, the pure egoless consciousness that exists beyond the senses of the mind. In this religion, they believe that in different forms, outside of the body, or indwelling, this spirit takes on different characteristics, or authorities, as it is manifested. One thing that hit me as a confirmation of Holy Spirit was the form of the *Adhiyagna*, which is referred to as the Witness, the Guide, the Bearer, the Enjoyer and the Great Lord; similar words used to describe the Holy Spirit of the Bible and Jesus. *Purusha* is also referred to as *Adhidaiva*, or the Supreme Divine, the Ancient, and the Omniscient, words to describe God the Father. Buddhism, Jainism and Sikhism all derive from Hinduism.

Long before Christianity hit Europe and the Americas during the slave trade, it was being practiced by many Africans as early as the late 1st century AD/early 2nd century AD in Northern Africa, but long before this, Africans practiced many forms of spirituality, not necessarily religion. All African spirituality points to a Supreme Being as Creator. Since there were so many languages and cultures in Africa, with differing practices and rituals, there is no way to point out, or claim, a certain "religious practice" of Africans; there were many. For the sake of this text, I researched the peoples and cultures of Nigeria and Ethiopia. *Odinani*, the traditional religion/philosophy of the Igbo people of Nigeria, is a theocentric belief system with the Supreme Being, *Chi ukwu* or *Chukwu* "God of Creation" at its head. In Igbo language, God may also be called *Chineke* "God who Creates" or "God and the Creator" (expressing a dual deity), depending on perspective. There are many similarities between the ancient African beliefs and modern-day, accepted forms of religion. The *Odinani* of Nigeria not only believed in a deity, but they also believed in a spiritual aspect of communication between Creator and creation. Africans communicated with ancestral spirits, those ancestors that died before them and felt they were carrying on their legacy, or destiny, through those left behind. Though many African tribes communicated with many different spirits, the *Odinani* did, however, believe in Spirits that were greater than the others. They referred to these Spirits as *Mmuo* and *Alusi*. We also see that from *Chineke*, the expression of God the Creator came the word *Chi*. *Chi* is considered the lower force of *Chukwu* and the only means to get connected to it since "no one reaches *Chukwu* directly or gets favor directly from the Supreme Force, except through *Chi*". This is similar to the Christian belief in Jesus' saying that "No one comes to the Father, but through Me." (John 14:6)

Ethiopia is considered to be the main hub of early Christianity in Africa. Dating back to 1st-7th Century A.D., and even well into the late first millennium B.C., Ethiopia had a rich legacy of spirituality. The Aksumite civilization originated and began to be populated in the fourth to third centuries B.C., developing into a kingdom between the mid-second century B.C. and the mid-second century A.D. Aksum (Axum), as it was known to the faithful of the Ethiopian Orthodox Church, is the place where the Arc of the Covenant was brought by Menelik I, son of the Queen of Sheba and King Solomon of Israel. The Arc of the Covenant, or the arc of the testimony, was a symbol of God's presence (His Spirit) amongst His people. It was first introduced to us in Exodus 25:

"And let them make me a sanctuary; that I may dwell among them. According to all that I shew thee, after the pattern of the tabernacle, and the pattern of all the instruments thereof, even so shall ye make it." (Verses 8-9, KJV)

"And there I will meet with thee, and I will commune with thee from above the mercy seat, from between the two cherubims which are upon the ark of the testimony, of all things which I will give thee in commandment unto the children of Israel." (Verse 22, KJV)

God has a way of bringing together nations in order to keep His covenant traveling throughout the generations. The Ethiopian tribes of Africa hold some of the most sacred beliefs and scripts of early Christendom and are very spiritual people. In fact, most of the Ethiopian worship pre-Christianity practiced is thought to be before the ancient Talmud was even written. The Ethiopian Orthodox Tewahedo Church was birthed, not out of evangelism, but initially, out of the heart of the King of Ethiopia. Most history

11

shows Christianity being birthed in the poor and outcast communities of the world, but not so in this region. It started by the request of a king. It sprung up and spread throughout the elite and wealthy of the kingdom first, then down into the inhabitants. There is something so powerful about this concept. When a leader of a nation accepts Jesus Christ as Lord and Savior, this nation is blessed and prospers greatly. Ethiopia is a very prosperous country to this day.

This church believes "God is one in three and three in one. The unity of God is neither convinced in the sense of an arithmetical digit nor of a solitary condition, but in that of an all-inclusive perfection. So the One is also eternally Three. He is, affirms the *Anaphora*, "three names and one God, three persona and one appearance, three persons and one essence".

The unity of the Godhead in Ethiopian culture is known as *Melekote*. God in three persons, referred to as *Akal*. They believe that "One was not before the other" and "the Second was not before the Third". They believe, in essence, in the Godhead: God the Father, God the Son and God the Holy Spirit. Listen to this prayer from an Ethiopian priest:

"But Thy living Holy Spirit knoweth the depth of Thy Godhead. He has declared to us Thy nature, and told us about Thy oneness. He taught Thy unity, and helped to know Thy Trinity."

We also know from Biblical scripture that a Eunuch from Ethiopia traveled to Jerusalem to worship the God of Israel and was met by Philip who later baptized the Eunuch. "And he arose and went: and, behold, a man of Ethiopia, an eunuch of great authority under Candace queen of the Ethiopians, who had the charge of all her treasure, and had come to Jerusalem for to worship," Acts 8:27

Ethiopia is still, to this day, very rich in its Christian beliefs and the Orthodox Church still holds firm belief in the Godhead.

Again, we know that communion between God and man was cut off when Adam disobeyed the Father in the Garden. Creator and Creation walked side by side in unbroken fellowship in the cool breeze of the day, basking in the glory of God's handiwork. His voice majestic and glistening with clarity, resounding through the plush and fruit-filled trees that spanned the Garden of Eden was Adam's reality. How did he feel when he could no longer hear the voice of his Creator? What agony and desperation he must have experienced in his disobedience. My heart aches as I try to fathom the separation of God and man.

Biblical and theological history records at least eleven hundred years before God speaks to another man so clearly, the man named Noah. For humanity not to hear the voice of God for thousands of years is unfathomable to me! What did humanity look like? Well, when the man Noah was summoned by Heaven, we are given a very clear account of the state of mankind. They were completely rebellious! God speaks to Noah to prepare an ark and that He was going to send a flood upon the earth that would wipe away all life, except for him and his family. Noah did not even know what "rain" was, as it had not before rained upon the earth in this manner. We know from the Garden of Eden that a "mist" sprang "up" from the Garden to sustain it, but there is no mention of anything falling down from the heavens, as God was now revealing to Noah. Rain, or water, is symbolic not only of cleansing, but of the Spirit of God. We will talk more about this in a later chapter. But Noah obeyed the voice of God and did as He commanded. God honored Noah's obedience and he and his family replenished the earth after the Flood.

At this time upon the earth, everyone spoke the same language. They were descendants of Noah and knew that he heard from God. They understood the relationship between him and the

Creator. I am sure Noah explicitly taught his children and grand-children the importance of intimacy with God and obedience to His voice. From Noah all throughout the Old Testament, we see men that heard the voice of God and were tested in their obedience to Him. It is a privilege to be able to hear His voice.

So again, we see many people from different cultures, back-grounds, religions and nations that have more in common than they are willing to acknowledge.

The indigenous American Indian spirituality is much the same as the ancient African spiritual practices. The land, the animals, and the elements of nature played a huge role in the spiritual development of Native American Indians. Their cultural practices were also very similar through spiritual dances, rituals, medicine men, and tribal leaders, or elders. Just as the African people, Native Americans had many names for God, but we will list just a few here. *Wakan Tanka* used primarily by the Lakota Indian Tribe, means Sacred Spirit. *Kitchi Manito* is referred to as the Great Spirit, or God. The Native Indian commandments from God are very similar to that of the Ten Commandments given to Moses on Mount Sinai. The native Indians of North America "spoke to the winds," which is an analogy of Holy Spirit in the Word of God. Listen to this prayer of the Native Americans:

Native American Prayer

Oh, Great Spirit
Whose voice I hear in the winds,
And whose breath gives life to all the world,
hear me, I am small and weak,
I need your strength and wisdom.

Let me walk in beauty
and make my eyes ever behold the red and purple sunset.
Make my hands respect the things you have made

and my ears sharp to hear your voice.
Make me wise so that I may understand
the things you have taught my people.
Let me learn the lessons you have
hidden in every leaf and rock.

I seek strength, not to be greater than my brother,
but to fight my greatest enemy- myself.
Make me always ready to come to you
with clean hands and straight eyes.
So when life fades, as the fading sunset,
my Spirit may come to you without shame.

- Chief Yellow Lark -
Lakota —

This prayer is very similar to any prayer a Christian would pray; from a human being that desires to do "good" and to please their Creator with their life. I was absolutely blown away in studying the various cultures and religions, as well as spiritual practices of humanity. I see that each of us has, in some way, been touched by the Godhead of Creation. My heart rejoices in the fact that God did not create a people to leave them alone to figure out this life on their own. His Creation is precious to Him, and He desires constant communication with them; to see His image and likeness formed in them and the extravagant love He had in creating them to be extended out towards humanity.

Holy Spirit is an intricate part of Creation and without Him; we would not be able to communicate with Father God. The Word of God says He will never leave us or forsake us. Though sin cut us off from direct communion with our Father, we see Holy Spirit activated and sent out on assignment in the lives of God's people after the fall of Adam. From Noah to Moses and from David to Jesus, Holy Spirit is seen throughout history reaching out to speak to God's people.

As we see Jesus leaving His earthly assignment, He empowers the disciples with these very words:

"Go therefore and make disciples of all the nations, baptizing them in the name of the Father and the Son and the Holy Spirit," Matthew 28:19

Not only do we see the Father confirming Holy Spirit in Creation, but we also see the Son, Jesus Christ, releasing Holy Spirit at His Ascension. Both Father and Son are affirming the assignment, the *person* of Holy Spirit, in the earth realm. How much more evidence do we need of this third person of the Godhead? Well, I am here on assignment, by the leading of Holy Spirit, to reveal Himself to you.

Paul, formerly known as Saul, the Roman soldier that persecuted and murdered thousands of Christians before he ran into the Light of the World and was completely transformed by the power of God, speaks with great authority, not only of God the Father, God the Son, but yes, also God the Holy Spirit. Paul was not one of the original disciples. He was not met by our Lord Jesus while He walked upon the earth. Jesus met Paul on the road to Damascus *in the Spirit* after His resurrection. Though Paul may have known "of" Jesus, He did not walk "with" Him, as did the disciples. This example of supernatural conversion spoke to me in such profound ways. All of the other disciples met Jesus personally and walked with Him, witnessed many miracles and sat and ate with Him. These men and women were able to physically touch our Lord and fellowship with Him, yet several of them doubted and denied Him at the Crucifixion. Paul, on the other hand, wanted to kill all of Jesus' followers, yet at the crossroads of persecution, on his way to murder even more followers; this soldier was met by the Living God Himself, *in the Spirit*. Though he was blinded physically, his spiritual eyes were miraculously opened by the Lord that day on the road to Damascus. This former persecutor rose to be one of the greatest voices on earth to proclaim Jesus Christ as the Messiah. I can only imagine the envy and persecution he, too, received from the other disciples. I can hear them now. How can this man that never walked with or touched "our" Lord who killed and imprisoned so many of "our" brothers and sisters speak with such power and authority? There is something so unique about a man that has been touched by the Spirit of God! Listen to the words of Jesus:

> "Jesus said to him, "Thomas, because you have *seen* Me, you have believed. Blessed are those who have *not seen* and yet have believed." John 20:29, emphasis

I believe this cannot be a truer statement of the Apostle Paul. He received the revelation of Jesus Christ by the Spirit of God, *Holy Spirit*. I believe our Lord was preparing a teaching moment for His disciples. I believe Saul, later named Paul, was a picture of how God wanted His disciples to believe and have faith in Him. Not merely by walking with Him, but when He was gone; when He was no longer able to be with them. God was preparing them. Paul infuriated many of the disciples, especially Peter, who was considered the one of "maturity;" the one who knew Jesus the greatest. Was it not Simon Peter that God spoke these words to, "And I also say to you that you are Peter, and on this rock I will build My church, and the gates of Hades shall not prevail against it." (Matthew 16:18) Jesus was speaking of Peter's faith, or revelation, of Him as the Son of the Living God. The only reason Jesus asked Peter to "Come," or *walk on the water*, was because it was on *this* faith that He would build His church. So for this Paul to walk in with no "history" with Jesus, and speaking with greater power than any of the disciples, including Peter, who did he think he was? Again, I firmly believe Paul was a "lesson" for Peter. Not only was God revealing the power of receiving Him by Holy Spirit, the Spirit of God, but He was also about to reveal to Peter that He not only wanted to save the Jewish people, but He also wanted the Gentiles. Oh what a wise God we serve! He will humble us in ways unimaginable for His Glory!

Another example of Paul's acknowledgement of Holy Spirit and the Godhead is in 2 Corinthians:

"The grace of the Lord Jesus Christ, and the love of God, and the fellowship of the Holy Spirit, be with you all."
2 Corinthians 13:14

He was speaking to the followers that were questioning his authority in Christ Jesus. Many were still rejecting Paul, but Holy Spirit was with him. He chose a spirit of gentleness with them, instead of outright rebuke and ended this letter with a reconfirming of the Godhead: Father, Son and Holy Spirit.

Here are just a few more scriptures that affirm Holy Spirit in relation to God:

"There is one body and one Spirit, just as also you were called in one hope of your calling; one Lord, one faith, one baptism, one God and Father of all who is over all and through all and in all." Ephesians 4:4-6

"But whenever a man turns to the Lord, the veil is taken away. Now the Lord is the Spirit; and where the Spirit of the Lord is, there is liberty. But we all, with unveiled face beholding as in a mirror the glory of the Lord, are being transformed into the same image from glory to glory, just as from the Lord, the Spirit." 2 Corinthians 3: 16-18

So, we see from these scriptural accounts that Holy Spirit is mentioned on the same plane as Father God, or the same level of authority. Father, Son and Holy Spirit were, and yet are, operating fully together in cohesiveness, in and out of time, to further God's plan in the earth realm. They are God's redemptive plan for mankind and operate strategically and in unison to carry out His purposes for His Creation. They neither contradict nor "step on one another's toes," if you will. They possess the same mind, the same heart and the same spirit, as they are One.

My heart grieves when I meet a follower of Christ that does not believe in Holy Spirit or refuses to acknowledge His person, or presence in their life. So many Christians are living defeated lives here in the earth realm, because they have rejected the third person of the Godhead. Many say that if you do not accept the full counsel of God's Word, then you are really not receiving any of it. I truly have to agree with this conclusion, especially in regards to Holy Spirit, because He is God! How can we Worship the Father if we reject His Spirit?

"But the hour is coming, and now is, when the true worshipers will worship the Father *in spirit and truth*; for the Father is seeking such to worship Him." John 4:23, emphasis

For centuries, man has taken it upon himself to translate, re-translate, take away, add to and outright reword the Holy Scriptures. Though I still believe in its authenticity as the inspired Word of God, I understand that I can never know the full intent of what God's heart is without the leading, guiding, directing and instructing of Holy Spirit. The Word says the letter kills, but the Spirit gives LIFE!

"Do we begin again to commend ourselves? Or do we need, as some others, epistles of commendation to you or letters of commendation from you? You are our epistle written in our hearts, known and read by all men; clearly you are an epistle of Christ, ministered by us, written not with ink but by the Spirit of the living God, not on tablets of stone but on tablets of flesh, that is, of the heart. And we have such trust through Christ toward God. Not that we are sufficient of ourselves to think of anything as being from ourselves, but our sufficiency is from God, who also made us sufficient as ministers of the new covenant, not of the letter but of the Spirit; for the letter kills, *but the Spirit gives life.*" 2 Corinthians 3: 1-6, emphasis

We must acknowledge His presence in our lives. We must seek to understand His assignment. We must activate His power and purpose in and through us if we are to walk fully in God's predestined plan for our lives. He was before...before you were formed in your mother's womb; He was at the drawing board of Creation mapping out your life. He has seen your entire life, before it was, so how can we reject His presence when His only desire is to speak to us, lead us through the windy roads of life, warn us of impending dangers and to help us reach our purpose in life? I witness too many Christians that believe they are going to Heaven, believe Jesus died and rose for their sins, but for the life of them cannot, or will not, acknowledge Holy Spirit. They are living defeated earthly lives when they have a Helper at their disposal. This should not be!

If you have yet to accept Him, I urge you to receive Him today. Ask Jesus to enter your heart and to forgive you of your sins. Ask Him to cleanse you, make you new and to be Lord of your life. You cannot receive Holy Spirit aside from Jesus Christ. Upon salvation, Holy Spirit enters our lives. Acknowledge His presence in your life as a necessity and allow Him to speak to you the things God desires for you to hear. You are not alone in this earth. God has provided a means to restore the broken fellowship between Creator and Creation, not only by the sacrifice of His only Son, Jesus Christ, but also through the breath of Life, the One found hovering over the face of the deep at Creation...*Holy Spirit.*

Smith Wigglesworth

"We must be careful not to choose, but to let God's Holy Spirit manage our lives; not to smooth down and explain away, but to stir up the gift and allow God's Spirit to disturb us and disturb us and disturb us until we yield and yield and yield and the possibility in God's mind for us becomes an established fact in our lives, with the rivers in evidence meeting the need of a dying world."

"Some people read their Bibles in Hebrew, some in Greek; I like to read mine in the Holy Ghost."
~Smith Wigglesworth

Chapter 2

The Person of Holy Spirit

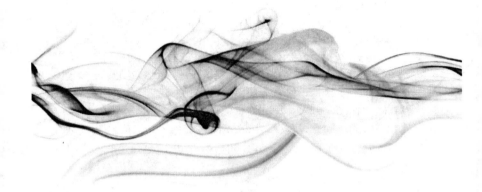

"In the beginning God created the heavens and the earth. The earth was without form and void; and darkness was on the face of the deep. And the Spirit of God was hovering over the face of the waters," Genesis 1: 1-2

Holy Spirit is not an *it*, not a *thing*; He is, indeed, God's Spirit, an entity, or person, with the authority of Father God backing Him. As we see from the above scripture, He was found "hovering" over the face of the waters, or the deep. We understand from Genesis 1:26 that God acknowledged His presence, Holy Spirit, as being "us," along with Jesus, in the creation of the earth and mankind. He not only confirmed that Holy Spirit was in the Beginning, but He also clearly states that this "us" was going to make man in "our" image, or likeness. This revelation extends to us the *person*, or *being* of Holy Spirit. Father God wanted us to know from the Beginning that Holy Spirit had full authority as a member of the Godhead, fully God, and fully Spirit.

It is clear that humanity refuses to accept what they cannot figure out. As we saw in the Prologue, unless we understand the definitions of certain words either in the dictionary or the historical, more dated, origins of them, we tend to shy away from or outright deny their authenticity. Spiritual things are often considered "spooky" or "far-fetched" by the majority of the populace. If we are afraid of something, we run away from it, instead of running to it. In this case, we are not running away from something, but ultimately, running away from God, in the *person* of Holy Spirit. The Bible says there is no fear in love and that perfect love casts out fear. (1 John 4:18) If we believe that God is merely the Creator, and not our Father, then we inherently separate relationship from the equation. We will view Him as a wrathful God, instead of a loving Father. So first, we must understand that we are created in Love *by* Love. He desires fellowship with His Creation. He loves us.

Secondly, we must understand that sin separated us from the Father; He cannot enter the earth realm in His fullness. The earth cannot contain the breadth, width, height and depth of His holiness. So, He chose to redeem the earth through His Son, Jesus Christ. He was fully man and fully God, operating in the full authority of Heaven on earth. Jesus, out of the realm of Heaven, heard from His Father through the voice of Holy Spirit in and through prayer. When our Lord walked with mankind on the face of the earth, He was the Word, or the Voice of God, to Creation. He was the conduit through which God revealed Himself to man. He was the Living Epistle, read by men. Upon His resurrection, before He ascended to Heaven, He commanded the disciples to wait for another. He urged them to remain in Jerusalem until He came unto them. Because they knew God as Father, and the Son as their Savior, these precious men and women could now receive the *person* of Holy Spirit as someone that was for them; someone that would help lead them by way of God's voice in the earth, *the Spirit within.*

Let's take a look at several scriptures that reveal the *person* of Holy Spirit in the lives of God's people:

> "Come near unto me, hear this: I have not spoken in secret from the beginning: from the time that it was, there am I: and now the Lord GOD, and His Spirit, hath sent me." Isaiah 48:16, KJV

> "I will declare the decree: The LORD hath said unto Me, Thou art my Son: this day have I begotten thee." Psalm 2:7, KJV

> "Now I urge you, brethren, by our Lord Jesus Christ and by the love of the Spirit, to strive together with me in your prayers to God for me." Romans 15:30

From these Scriptures, we clearly see the "personalizing," or *relational* qualities of Holy Spirit, even *communicational*, giving us something real to connect with personally. The Word says that He will never leave us nor forsake us. (Deuteronomy 31:6) I firmly believe this is indicative of Holy Spirit's attributes and assignment in our lives. Once we see Him as a *person* and not a ghost-like figure or apparition, we can now allow ourselves to draw closer to the voice of God in our lives.

All throughout the Word of God, Holy Spirit is mentioned; in the Old Testament and the New Covenant. Again, it baffles me that so many try to exclude His voice from scripture and claim He is non-existent, but we will deal with the "spirit" behind this deception in a later chapter. Follow me on this journey in getting to know the authentic *person* of Holy Spirit.

The preaching of the Gospel is about ninety-nine percent re-sponsible for the way in which we view scripture. This should not be, but it is, indeed, true in the majority of cases. Religion and tradition play a huge role in how God, Jesus and yes, Holy Spirit are not only portrayed, but also in how they are perceived, as well as received. If we preach that God is Creator and Jesus is the Redeemer, but leave out the importance of the work of Holy Spirit in our lives, then all we are seeking is Heaven. Our work on earth is the furthest thing from our hearts and minds. I speak with many people that have been in church their entire lives, but have *yet* to hear a message preached on Holy Spirit. And some, though they know it is in the Word of God, *choose* not to even speak upon His role in their lives. Others, because of tradition, view Him as an *it*, instead of a *person*, and never internalize the relational aspects of His character. This grieves me deeply, as I have come to truly understand the need for His presence in my everyday life.

Before I received Holy Spirit into my life, truly acknowledged His presence at work in and through me, I was an immature follower of Christ. There always seemed to be something missing, and I could not put my finger upon it. I was saved, but there still remained a huge void in my life.

"The Spirit Himself bears witness with our spirit that we are children of God," Romans 8:16

Growing up in a Methodist church, I heard the Word of God preached, but never heard a message about Holy Spirit? I was not even taught about a real, personal relationship with Jesus Christ; only that Heaven was real, Hell was real, Jesus died so we could go to Heaven and that was pretty much it. So, when I gave my life to Jesus at the age of twelve, it wasn't because I knew He absolutely loved and adored me and wanted to redeem my life, but that it was the right thing to do. I did not run into this unconditional love, until I was twenty-two years old and I have not looked back since. I knew God loved me. I knew He revealed that love through the sacrifice of His only Son, Jesus Christ who showed me through His selflessness that He, too, loved me dearly. But I did not know this "third *person*" that I read about. Even though I believed I was loved and confessed my sins and received forgiveness from God, it was still inconceivable that He would allow this "mess" of a woman into Heaven? I battled with those feelings of guilt and unworthiness for several years.

In January of 2003, both my husband and I made the decision to ask "the" Holy Spirit into our lives. Our experience was not so much a *traditional* one, as the church we joined was a Spirit-filled atmosphere that openly displayed impartation through the laying on of hands. Some churches believe that if hands are not laid on someone, then they have not received Holy Spirit. First, let's go back to what I mentioned earlier in that the moment we accept Jesus Christ as our Lord and Savior, Holy Spirit is activated in our lives. But because most churches don't preach this, we think it should be an altogether separate event in the life of a follower of Jesus Christ. This is doctrinal error. So, many receive, or acknowledge, Holy Spirit many, many years after their salvation and some, sadly, never do in their lifetime.

For me, it was almost an instantaneous change in my walk with the Lord. I began seeing and hearing the Word of God in a different way. I received the revelation of *who* He really was, and that He was not an *it*, but an intricate piece to the puzzle of my life; my entire walk with God shifted. I now understood the above scripture, but this time, it became personal to me. The Spirit *Himself* was bearing witness with my spirit that I was, indeed, a child of God. My doubts, fears, insecurities and guilt began to dissipate and I began taking the Word of God at face value, and Holy Spirit was a crucial part of this journey. He became real to me, and from that moment on, I have stopped referring to Him as "the" Holy Spirit, but in fact *Holy Spirit*, the Spirit of the Living God within me. There is no greater revelation other than that of Jesus Christ as the Son of the Living God! I am grateful to Father God for opening my eyes and my heart to His Truth. I am not sure where my life would be had I not received His precious Holy Spirit.

In recognizing Holy Spirit as a *person*, many seek proof, from scripture, as to why we can undoubtedly believe such things. Well, I am glad there are at least some that will earnestly seek for the Truth. A person is someone made up of feelings, emotions, characteristics and attributes. They are able to think, speak, feel and have an awareness of things around them. If something is considered inanimate, it cannot possess such things. Holy Spirit, all throughout the Word of God, is seen as possessing the qualities of a living, breathing entity. Scripture describes Holy Spirit as "He," "Himself," and "Who," all references to a living being. And we see clearly Him feeling with emotion, just as we do.

"But they rebelled and *grieved* His Holy Spirit; Therefore, He turned Himself to become their enemy, He fought against them." Isaiah 63:10, emphasis

grieve

This says He was *grieved.* The word grieve is a very strong word. It means to suffer grief, grief being deep sorrow, misery, torment, anguish, heartbreak, woe or despair. It speaks of mourning. How can "something" so unnecessary to followers of Christ in the scheme of scripture *feel* like mankind? So deeply? Because what we fail to understand is that He is, indeed, God. We cannot separate them; they are One in the same. Let's search out the scriptures a little further.

"Now I urge you, brethren, by our Lord Jesus Christ and by the love of the Spirit, to strive together with me in your prayers to God for me." Romans 15:30

Love is something most preachers preach about. For us to come into the saving knowledge of Jesus Christ, we are taught of God's love for us. In fact, His love is His attribute. The Word of God says, "He who does not love does not know God, for God *is* love." (1 John 4:8, emphasis) And of course, any one raised in the church as a child can recite the love verse of God in the sacrifice of His Son, Jesus Christ, "For God so loved the world that He gave

His only begotten Son, that whoever believes in Him should not perish but have everlasting life." (John 3:16) Jesus exemplified Love as He hung on the Cross, redeeming us from the curse of sin. But how many of us know of, or have read, scriptures that reveal the love of Holy Spirit? Again, He strives alongside of the Father and the Son in the *same* heart. For Him to grieve, He must have deep feelings, or emotions, for God's people. Someone can't truly grieve you or cause you deep sorrow or anguish if you are not in relationship with them, or have some sort of investment in them. Holy Spirit has great investment in God's people and just because we refuse to acknowledge Him does not mean that He does not exist or that He will just go away. In fact, He strives incessantly to let us know He is with us and for us.

There are five references to the "names" of Holy Spirit in the Word of God. Let's look at them:

❖ The Spirit of God
❖ The Spirit of Christ
❖ The Spirit of Your Father
❖ The Spirit of Truth
❖ The Spirit of the Lord

1. **The Spirit of God**: "However, you are not in the flesh but in the Spirit, if indeed the Spirit of God dwells in you." Romans 8:9a

As we stated earlier, to be born again, as a child of God, we are subsequently born of the Spirit. We exchange the lusts of the flesh with the power of the Spirit. He enables us to walk in the Spirit. But if we walk in the flesh we cannot please Father God.

2. **The Spirit of Christ**: "But if anyone does not have the Spirit of Christ, he does not belong to Him." Romans 8:9b

God reveals in this scripture that if we do not have the Spirit of Christ, then we, in no way, know Him or belong to Him. He does not consider us His. So, it is paramount that we accept Jesus into our lives to live eternally with Father God.

3. **The Spirit of Your Father**: "For it is not you who speak, but it is the Spirit of your Father who speaks in you." Matthew 10:20

We are encouraged that even in our times of greatest persecution; we should not worry about what we will say. He will give us the very words to speak and they will come through the conduit of the Spirit of Your Father, Holy Spirit.

4. **The Spirit of Truth**: "that is the Spirit of truth, whom the world cannot receive, because it does not behold Him or know Him, but you know Him because He abides with you, and will be in you." John 14:17

We have a gift the world does not have. Truth is something many say they possess, and many boast of obtaining, but aside from God, Jesus Christ, and Holy Spirit, they have nothing! The Truth is not in them, nor do they know the Truth. We have Him living on the inside. We have what the world seeks.

5. **The Spirit of the Lord**: "And when they came up out of the water, the Spirit of the Lord snatched Philip away; and the eunuch saw him no more, but went on his way rejoicing." Acts 8:39

Supernatural occurrences were seen greatly in Biblical days. Several people are recorded as being "caught up," "snatched," or "translated" by the Spirit of the Lord. This is Holy Spirit being used by God in the earth.

We must learn to receive His presence in our lives, but more importantly, accept Him for who He truly is and to come into relationship with Him, so we grow closer in fellowship. His character, or attributes, further reveals the mind of Holy Spirit. His design is absolute intelligence. He opens up the heart of God for our lives and leads, directs, instructs and reveals as He wills.

"For what man knows the things of a man except the spirit of the man which is in him? Even so no one knows the things of God except the Spirit of God." 1 Corinthians 2:11

As we found out earlier, we can believe in God and accept Jesus as Lord, but if we refuse to acknowledge Holy Spirit in our lives, we are absolutely lost. We will go through life batting at the air trying to find our way through the maze of existence. It is devastating to know that we had the *person* of Holy Spirit available to us, but yet we never had the opportunity to receive Him into our lives, because we were never taught about Him. The Word of God is *full* of the unique attributes of Holy Spirit.

1. He Comforts (2 Corinthians 1:4)
2. He Fills (Ephesians 5:18)
3. He Calls (Acts 13:2)
4. He Prays (Romans 8:26)
5. He Helps (John 16:17)
6. He Reveals (1 Corinthians 2:10)
7. He Instructs (1 John 2:27)
8. He Guides (John 16:13)
9. He Leads (Matthew 4:1)
10. He Speaks (Matthew 10:20)
11. He Teaches (1 Corinthians 2:13)
12. He Testifies (Romans 8:16)
13. He Prophesies (2 Peter 1:21)
14. He Renews (Ephesians 4:23)
15. He Restores (Psalm 51:12)
16. He Offers Freedom (2 Corinthians 3:17)

17. He Transforms (2 Corinthians 3:18)
18. He Frees (Romans 8:2)
19. He Strengthens (Ephesians 3:16)
20. He Fills (Micah 3:8)
21. He Lives In Us (1 Corinthians 3:16)
22. He Bears Witness (John 15:26)
23. He Helps Us Obey (Galatians 5:16)
24. He Brings Joy (Romans 14:17)
25. He Empowers (Acts 1:8)
26. He Cast Out Demons (Matthew 12:28)
27. He Unites (1 Corinthians 12:3)
28. He Sanctifies (1 Peter 1:2)
29. He Provides Access to God (Ephesians 2:18)
30. He Enables (1 Corinthians 2:12)
31. He Encourages (Matthew 10:19)
32. He Seals (2 Corinthians 1:22)
33. He Assists (Romans 8:26)
34. He Aids (John 14:16)
35. He Knows (1 Corinthians 2:10)
36. He Appoints (Acts 20:28)
37. He Witnesses (Romans 8:16)
38. He Intercedes (Romans 8:27)
39. He Gives Life (John 6:63)
40. He Baptizes (Matthew 28:19)
41. He Forbids (Acts 16:6)
42. He Corrects (2 Timothy 3:16)
43. He Rebukes (2 Timothy 3:16)
44. He Searches (1 Corinthians 2:10)
45. He is Truth (John 16:13)
46. He is Received (Galatians 3:2)
47. He is Given (Acts 5:32)
48. He Grieves (Ephesians 4:30)
49. He Loves (Romans 5:5)
50. He Has a Mind (1 Corinthians 2:11)
51. He Dwells Within Us (1 Corinthians 3:16)
52. He Tests (1 John 4:1)

53. He Judges (John 16:8)
54. He Fellowships (2 Corinthians 13:14)
55. He Makes Us Holy (2 Thessalonians 2:13)
56. He Regenerates (Titus 3:5)
57. He Seeks (John 4:23)
58. He Anoints (1 John 2:20)
59. He Authors (2 Peter 1:20-21)
60. He Counsels (John 14:26)
61. He Advocates (John 14:26)
62. He Convicts (John 16:8)
63. He Endows (1 Corinthians 12:4)
64. He Draws (John 6:44)
65. He Enables Us to Produce Fruit (Galatians 5:22-25)

This is surely not an exhaustive list of the attributes or characteristics of Holy Spirit, but just gives us an idea of the magnitude of His personality in relation to mankind.

The personality of Holy Spirit is usually questioned because we are prone to think of Him as an influence, a power, a manifestation or influence of the Divine nature, or an agent, rather than a *Person*. There is too much Scripture that solidifies His existence as the Spirit of God Himself. There are other characteristics Holy Spirit is known by that relates outside of personal attribution. Let's look at a few:

The Breath: "And when He had said this, He breathed on them, and said to them, "Receive the Holy Spirit." John 20:22

The Wind: "When the Day of Pentecost had fully come, they were all with one accord in one place. And suddenly there came a sound from heaven, as of a rushing mighty wind, and it filled the whole house where they were sitting." Acts 2:1-2

The Power: "And Jesus returned to Galilee in the power of the Spirit, and news about Him spread through all the surrounding district." Luke 4:14

The Fire: "Then there appeared to them divided tongues, as of fire, and one sat upon each of them. And they were all filled with the Holy Spirit and began to speak with other tongues, as the Spirit gave them utterance." Acts 2:3-4

The Water: "Most assuredly, I say to you, unless one is born of water and the Spirit, he cannot enter the kingdom of God." John 3:5

The Oil: "But you have an anointing from the Holy One, and you know all things." 1 John 2:20

The Dove: "When He had been baptized, Jesus came up immediately from the water; and behold, the heavens were opened to Him, and He saw the Spirit of God descending like a dove and alighting upon Him." Matthew 3:16

Other names associated with Holy Spirit:

- THE SPIRIT OF GRACE: Hebrews 10:29 – "And hath done despite unto the Spirit of grace."
- THE SPIRIT OF JUDGMENT/BURNING: Isaiah 4:4 – "When the Lord shall have washed away the filth of the daughters of Zion.... by the spirit of judgment and the spirit of burning."
- THE SPIRIT OF LIFE: Romans 8:2 – "For the law of the Spirit of life in Christ Jesus hath made me free from the law of sin and death."
- THE SPIRIT OF WISDOM AND KNOWLEDGE: Isaiah 11:2–"The Spirit of the LORD shall rest upon Him, The Spirit of wisdom and understanding, The

Spirit of counsel and might, The Spirit of kno

o-

and of the fear of the LORD."

- THE SPIRIT OF PROMISE: Ephesians 1:13 – "You were sealed with that Holy Spirit of promise."
- THE SPIRIT OF GLORY: 1 Peter 4:14 – "The spirit of glory and of God rests upon you."

So, we see there are not just a few characteristics, or personality traits, attributed to Holy Spirit. He is seen all throughout the canons of Scripture from the inception of Creation to the Second Coming of our Lord and Savior Jesus Christ. He was in the Beginning and is in the End. He can be as real to you in this earth as the *person* standing next to you if you allow His presence to saturate your entire life. To know Him is truly one of the greatest gifts from God!

We are able to see the many roles Holy Spirit plays in conjunction with God and with Jesus Christ in the renewal, restoration and redemption of mankind. All three *Persons* are truly divine, yet eternally distinct from one another. His presence is absolutely imperative to the inner workings of humanity. As we read these scriptures, we can begin to know Holy Spirit better. God is drawing us by Holy Spirit. It we reject the working of the Spirit of God in our lives, as followers of Christ; we are missing a crucial piece to the puzzle of our spiritual lives. We will truly live defeated lives not understanding His precious character, personality and attributes that are designed to carry us through this life. He is our Divine Guide, our spiritual GPS; He leads us by design as we submit to following Him. No longer do we have to be bound by fear or even distance; He is here for us. He needs no introduction, but He absolutely needs an invitation. Ask Him into your life today. He is the Promise Left for the Believer...*Holy Spirit.*

Katherine Khulman

"It was in Franklin, Pennsylvania in the old Billy Sunday Tabernacle. I had gone to Franklin by faith (1946), not knowing what I would find there. It was in the third service, as I was preaching on the Holy Spirit, sharing with the people the little that I knew about that Third **Person** of the Trinity - a woman stood up and testified to her healing of a tumor."

"It's the Holy Spirit; IT'S WHAT THE HOLY SPIRIT DOES THROUGH A YIELDED VESSEL."
~Katherine Khulman

Chapter 3
The Purpose of Holy Spirit

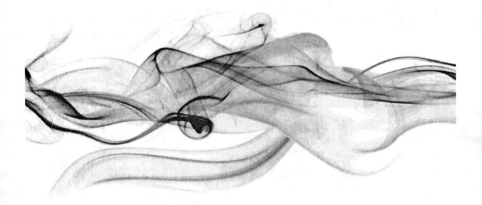

"And when He has come, He will convict the world of sin, and of righteousness, and of judgment: of sin, because they do not believe in Me; of righteousness, because I go to My Father and you see Me no more; of judgment, because the ruler of this world is judged." John 16:8

Holy Spirit has a job description. In reading Scripture, you can count on finding clear descriptions of the Spirit's various tasks. Scripture does not leave the works of the Spirit to our imagination. The Spirit of God has specific work to be done, and Scripture clearly teaches us about that work. He has an assignment just as our Lord and Savior Jesus Christ had in the earth. In the Beginning, God created the heavens and the earth: "The Age of Creation". Jesus was sent to redeem the earth from the curse of sin,

"The Age of the Son". Now, after our Lord ascended into Heaven, the Promise of Holy Spirit is the dispensation we currently enjoy. The age we are in is known as the "Age of Grace," or the "Age of the Spirit".

Creation

In *Creation,* Holy Spirit was found "hovering over the waters".

"The earth was without form, and void; and darkness was on the face of the deep. And the Spirit of God was hovering over the face of the waters." Genesis 1:2

As a little child, I had many dreams of "hovering" over scenes and backdrops in various places. I felt like I was enormous, because I could see a panoramic view of each location I entered. This view not only gave me access, but it provided me insight into the areas I was being afforded the privilege of viewing. It was strategic and I was able to see things I normally would not have been able to see. I found out much later on in my life that this was a gift God had given me at a very early age, yet I did not understand its purpose or power, until the appointed time God needed me to fully understand, when I received Holy Spirit. I was being granted "access" into the Spiritual realm through insight, oversight, illumination and revelation; the gift of the prophetic realm.

Holy Spirit had, and still has, full access into the earthly realm. I believe the knowledge of Him hovering over the waters revealed God's intelligent design and purpose for this third person of the Godhead. He was a part of the *Creation* of the Universe. His input was crucial and His knowledge, invaluable.

"You send forth Your Spirit, they are *created*; And You *renew* the face of the earth." Psalm 104:30, emphasis

"By the word of the Lord were the heavens *made*, their starry host by the *breath of his mouth*" Psalm 33:6, emphasis

Holy Spirit not only played an important role in the *Creation* of the heavens and the earth, but He also stood proudly at the inauguration of mankind.

"Then God said, "Let Us make man in *Our* image, according to *Our* likeness; let them have dominion over the fish of the sea, over the birds of the air, and over the cattle, over all the earth and over every creeping thing that creeps on the earth." Genesis 1:26, emphasis

Let's listen to Job's declaration of this Life giving Spirit:

"The Spirit of God has *made* me, and the *breath of the Almighty* has given me life." Job 33:4, emphasis

"By His Spirit He *adorned* the heavens; His hand pierced the fleeing serpent." Job 26:13, emphasis

My God! His presence is creative!

Salvation

Salvation is inexplicably credited to the birth, life, death and resurrection of our Lord and Savior, Jesus Christ. It was His ultimate sacrifice as the Lamb of God that secured the right for us to live eternally with Him, as we submit and surrender our lives and accept His as our own. But what role does Holy Spirit play in this life transforming decision? We saw above that He was in Creation, and it is credible to assume He knew God's plan to send His Son as the Redeemer of the world. He, too, would be a part of this assignment. Holy Spirit awakens in man a deep hidden awareness of guilt. He convinces man of sin, even when there was no consciousness of sin previously. Holy Spirit uses the Word of God preached and touches the heart of the hearer, making it accessible to the Word. As our eyes and hearts are opened, through the Word, Holy Spirit will draw us to repentance.

"No one can come to Me unless the Father who sent Me *draws* him; and I will raise him up at the last day." John 6:44, emphasis

We understand that God can do nothing in the earth today, unless it is through Holy Spirit. So when it says the Father *draws*, this represents Holy Spirit. And it is also important to point out here that God's "drawing" is His predestined will.

Justification

Many view salvation and justification as the same thing. In some instances, they absolutely represent the same thing. But let's dig a little deeper into what this act means for the Believer. *Justification* is an act of God that pardons, accepts and declares a sinner "just" on the basis of Christ's righteousness. What this revelation does is takes the burden off of us as "sinners," in thinking we have to work to receive salvation. *Justification* is given by grace, which is dispersed by the Spirit of God, *Holy Spirit.*

Justification is a one-time act that is deemed complete, unlike sanctification, which is an ongoing process in the life of Christians. We are engrafted into the family of God through the Will of our Father in Heaven, by the imputation of our sins upon our Lord Jesus Christ and through the witness of Holy Spirit.

"The Spirit Himself bears witness with our spirit that we are children of God, and if children, then heirs—heirs of God and joint heirs with Christ, if indeed we suffer with Him, that we may also be glorified together." Romans 8:16-17

Adoption

"For you did not receive the spirit of bondage again to fear, but you received the Spirit of adoption by whom we cry out, 'Abba, Father.' The Spirit Himself bears witness with our spirit that we are children of God," Romans 8:15-16

So many in the world today are fatherless, whether by choice or by unsuspecting circumstances. Our world is broken in many ways due to the lack of fathers present in the lives of their children. Many children lack identity, because the father imparts something very unique that cannot be replaced by a mother, or even a guardian. When a father has a son, he is elated, because he now has a name carrier; someone that can carry his name through the generations. In broken homes and even homes where the parents are not married, some mothers choose to change their children's last name, or not even give their children this privilege. In their ignorance, or immaturity, they fail to realize this is a part of their identity. It is who they are, yet they are stripped of this due to great selfishness.

"But when the fullness of the time had come, God sent forth His Son, born of a woman, born under the law, to redeem those who were under the law, that we might receive the adoption as sons. And because you are sons, God has sent forth the Spirit of His Son into your hearts, crying out, 'Abba, Father!' Therefore you are no longer a slave but a son, and if a son, then an heir of God through Christ." Galatians 4:4-7

Many children around the world are without father and mother, either homeless or in the foster care system, awaiting adoption. Their lives are empty and void. Without that identity, many find themselves searching in all the wrong places for validation. I know this feeling of helplessness and hopelessness. Though I had my father for the first fourteen years of my life, after his death, I lost a huge part of me. I tried to take my life; the pain was unbearable. Fortunately, God saved my life. But the void was still there. For eight years, I walked through great darkness, seeking the love and stability my father provided in my life. Needless to say, I would find it in no other place than the arms of another father, my Heavenly Father. He mended and filled the hole in my heart and my life has never been the same since.

The name *Abba* simply means "father". His desire is to fill the void in our lives and to give us a Heavenly legacy, and this *adoption* comes through the vestibule of Holy Spirit. It is by the Spirit of God that we cry, "Abba, Father!" What child does not want to hear and feel the love of a father? Father God is waiting, standing by, for whoever will call upon the name of His Son, Jesus Christ to receive the Spirit of *Adoption*. Though we are assured an exchange from earthly father to Heavenly Father, there is a promise in Malachi 4 of an earthly restoring of fathers and children.

"Behold, I will send you Elijah the prophet before the coming of the great and dreadful day of the LORD: And he will turn the hearts of the fathers to the children, and the hearts of the children to their fathers, lest I come and strike the earth with a curse." Malachi 4:5-6

What a picture of Restoration and Reconciliation for God's people!

Regeneration

The next phase of purpose we will look at is *Regeneration*. Regeneration is known as the action or process of regenerating or being regenerated, in particular, the formation of new animal or plant tissue. The Biblical definition is the spiritual transformation in a person, brought about by the Holy Spirit that brings the individual from being spiritually dead to become a spiritually alive human being. Regeneration is another way of speaking about the new birth or the second birth or being born again.[ii]

So we see here that not only was Holy Spirit a valuable and strategic part of the earthly Creation, as well as man, and the drawing to salvation and spiritual adoption, but He is also a major factor in the "new creation," or the *Regeneration* of the spiritual birth. What a glorious view of His placement and purpose in the journey of mankind!

42

"Jesus answered, 'Most assuredly, I say to you, unless one is born of water and the Spirit, he cannot enter the kingdom of God. That which is born of the flesh is flesh, and that which is born of the Spirit is spirit. Do not marvel that I said to you, 'You must be born again.' The wind blows where it wishes, and you hear the sound of it, but cannot tell where it comes from and where it goes. So is everyone who is born of the Spirit." John 3:5-8

This spiritual work of *Regeneration* cannot be obtained without the aid of Holy Spirit. So I submit to you, get to know Him today. Just because you refuse to believe in Him, does not mean He is not there. He is, indeed, very real and a very strategic part of the purpose in your regenerative process. Again, once you repent of your sins and ask Jesus to be Lord of your life, Holy Spirit is activated within you. His Spirit lives in you. But if you never utilize the power of God within you, then how can you live a life of victory in Jesus Christ? I think there is much we need to reconsider concerning Holy Spirit if we are to call ourselves followers of Christ.

Let's look at Holy Spirit's purpose in the life of Jesus in the earth. If we can believe that Holy Spirit came upon Mary and she conceived the Son of God, Jesus, how can we not believe He, Holy Spirit, is still available and active in our everyday lives? We cannot pick and choose the parts of the Bible we want to believe and not believe. It is the full counsel of God's Word or it is none at all. The Word of God says not to add to or take away any portion of the inspired Word (Revelation 2:19), which is given by none other than...*Holy Spirit*.

"And so we have the prophetic word confirmed, which you do well to heed as a light that shines in a dark place, until the day dawns and the morning star rises in your hearts; knowing this first, that no prophecy of Scripture is of any private interpretation, for prophecy never came by the will of man, but holy men of God spoke as they were moved by the Holy Spirit." 2 Peter 1:18-21

When God called me to write in the year 2000, I was extremely intimidated. Now don't get me wrong, anyone that knows me would probably burst out laughing at this statement, because I have been "known" to write novels out of everything from love letters to blogs. This was different. I knew God was calling me to write as Holy Spirit led my pen. He clearly commanded me to be led, or inspired, by Holy Spirit. I would sit for hours in my office in Germany and pray, asking Holy Spirit for the Words He needed His people to hear. When I didn't hear anything, I put my pen down. When I received a strong pull in my spirit, I would get up and go over to my "writing desk" and my pen would not stop, until He stopped speaking. All of my books, so far, have been written as Holy Spirit moved upon me to write. Funny, all of them have been written within three months, literally. This one, however, has taken three years to come to fruition. There must be something to this *Holy Spirit!*

It is not difficult for me to imagine the writers of the Bible being moved by Holy Spirit to write the Word of God. For the past sixteen years, this has been my reality. I am sure I will write more books in the future, some that will be more of my experience than of inspiration, but I am a living witness that Holy Spirit is living, breathing and is, indeed, a major player in the purpose for which God has created me. I have been born-again, of the water and of the Spirit and He is leading me every step of the way! He has transformed my life. I cannot do this without Him!

Holy Spirit *regenerates* us. God formed man from the dust of the ground and breathed into his nostrils the Breath of Life and man became a living being. Our existence would not be possible if it were not for Holy Spirit! Each and every day you wake up and take a deep breath, remember it is *He* who breathes through you.

Sanctification

The process a follower of Christ goes through is seen by many as cumbersome. "Does it take all of that?" Yes, it does. We are human; we want the Blessing of God without obedience to His Word. If we can get something without having to do too much work, we will, most likely, take the shortcuts. There are no shortcuts in God. God knows us better than we know ourselves. He sees our future before we even get there; therefore, He knows how long it will take each of us to walk in His fullness, in spiritual maturity.

Sanctification is the act or process of acquiring sanctity, of being made or becoming holy. The Biblical meaning refers to being "set apart" for special use or purpose, that is, to make holy or sacred. This walk with Christ is not a sprint, but a marathon. More than God wants us to have what we want, He desires we are transformed into His image and likeness; that His attributes are formed within us, Christ-likeness. This process of being "made holy" is really a lifetime work in the life of a follower of Christ. As we meditate upon His holy Word, we grow daily in His image, as the flesh progressively falls away, the Spirit leads us into Truth.

"But we are bound to give thanks to God always for you, brethren beloved by the Lord, because God from the beginning chose you for salvation through sanctification by the Spirit and belief in the truth," 2 Thessalonians 2:13

Another aspect of *Sanctification* is the state of being "set apart" for the Lord. As we allow the Word of God to transform and renew our minds, Holy Spirit works alongside of the Word to guard, or sanctify, us in this ever changing, evil world. God desires to "show off" His children to the world, not in pride or arrogance, but in His light and in His love *through* us. He wants them to see that He is able to turn around even the most devastating of situations for His glory. Let's look at several instances of Holy Spirit at work through *Sanctification*:

Leviticus 11:44 – "...Consecrate yourselves therefore, and be holy, for I am holy. ..."

Matthew 5:48 – "You therefore must be perfect, as your heavenly Father is perfect."

Romans 6:22 – "But now that you have been set free from sin and have become slaves of God, the fruit you get leads to sanctification and its end, eternal life."

1 Corinthians 6:11 – "...But you were washed, you were sanctified, you were justified in the name of the Lord Jesus Christ and by the Spirit of our God."

2 Corinthians 3:18 – "And we all, with unveiled face, beholding the glory of the Lord, are being transformed into the same image from one degree of glory to another. For this comes from the Lord who is the Spirit."

2 Corinthians 7:1 – "...beloved, let us cleanse ourselves from every defilement of body and spirit, bringing holiness to completion in the fear of God."

1 Thessalonians 4:3– "For this is the will of God, your sanctification..."

1 Thessalonians 4:7– "For God has not called us for impurity, but in holiness."

1 Thessalonians 5:23–"Now may the God of peace himself sanctify you completely, and may your whole spirit and soul and body be kept blameless at the coming of our Lord Jesus Christ."

Hebrews 6:1–"Therefore let us leave the elementary doctrine of Christ and go on to maturity..."

Hebrews 12:14–"Strive for peace with everyone, and for the holiness without which no one will see the Lord."

James 1:4 – "And let steadfastness have its full effect, that you may be perfect and complete, lacking in nothing."

1 Peter 1:15-16–"...but as he who called you is holy, you also be holy in all your conduct, since it is written, "You shall be holy, for I am holy...""

1 John 4:18–"There is no fear in love, but perfect love casts out fear. For fear has to do with punishment, and whoever fears has not been perfected in love."

Glorification

Wow! Did you know Holy Spirit is a part of all of this? Not many do, and many others refuse to study the existence of the Spirit of God in the scheme of humanity. From salvation to sanctification, Holy Spirit is leading us every step of the way. The last process I want to discuss is *Glorification*. *Glorification* is considered the final stage of sanctification, or the final removal of sin from a Believer's life.

"For I consider that the sufferings of this present time are not worthy to be compared with the glory which shall be revealed in us." Romans 8:18

" For our light affliction, which is but for a moment, is working for us a far more exceeding and eternal weight of glory," 2 Corinthians 4:17

It is the coming of our Lord that will usher in His ultimate glory over our lives. In the earth realm, we hear of His glory being revealed, or of His glory being upon us. This comes through us living holy lives here on the earth and being transformed daily into the image and likeness of God through Christ Jesus. It is the outward transformation of an inward change, whereas the world is able to see the "light" of Jesus within us, and subsequently surrender their lives unto Him.

"Let your light so shine before men, that they may see your good works and glorify your Father in heaven." Matthew 5:16

This glory is not for us, but for Him! The Word of God says He will share His glory with no man!

"I am the LORD: that is my name: and my glory will I not give to another, neither my praise to graven images." Isaiah 42:8, KJV

So, we see what the glory of the Lord is and what it is for, or rather *Who* it is for. *Glorification* is an instantaneous transformation not for God necessarily, but for the Believer, and Holy Spirit is an intricate part of this glorious process!

"For the grace of God that brings salvation has appeared to all men, teaching us that, denying ungodliness and worldly lusts, we should live soberly, righteously, and godly in the present age, looking for the blessed hope and glorious appearing of our great God and Savior Jesus Christ," Titus 2:10-13

Upon the return of our Lord and Savior, Jesus Christ, we will be transformed into our glorious bodies, we will see Him "as He is," according to the Word of God (1 John 3:2), but until then, we are in a process of sanctification, as we saw earlier, preparing us for that Glorious Day!

"But we all, with unveiled face, beholding as in a mirror the glory of the Lord, are being transformed into the same image from glory to glory, just as by the *Spirit of the Lord*." 2 Corinthians 3:18, emphasis

Holy Spirit is like our *midwife*. He walks with us every step of the way, helping us and leading us in the birthing not only of holiness in our lives, but also of our purpose. When the culmination of sanctification has come, we will be thrust out of the womb of sin and adversity and delivered into the heavenly and glorious presence of Father God! My Lord! He will finally be glorified in our heavenly bodies and we will have eternal access to His presence. Do you now see the absolute significance of Holy Spirit in your life? Let us go on further.

Here are several other instances where Holy Spirit was used in carrying out the Will of Father God in the ministry of our Lord Jesus Christ:

- He was Conceived by Holy Spirit, born of the Spirit, Luke 1:35
- He was Led by the Spirit, Matthew 4:1
- He was Anointed by the Spirit for Service, Acts 10:38
- He was Crucified in the Power of the Spirit, Hebrews 9:14
- He was Raised by the Power of the Spirit, Romans 1:4; 8:11
- He gave Commandment to His Disciples and Church Through the Spirit, Acts 1:2
- He is the Bestower of Holy Spirit, Acts 2:33

Holy Spirit's purpose is not one-fold, two-fold or even three-fold; His assignment goes beyond human comprehension. For someone not to believe in Him, or believe He exists is unfathomable for one, with so much scripture to back Him, and two, the supernatural things we see God performing in our lives that we have no answer for. He is *always* working, even when we don't know it. He is orchestrating plans and purposes from Father God, weaving and intermingling circumstances and situations, so that God's Will is done in and through our lives. He is HOLY SPIRIT!

More examples of Holy Spirit's purpose:

1. **Holy Spirit exalts Jesus.** Nowhere do we see Holy Spirit exalting Himself; He is always seen lifting up the name of Jesus, leading us to receive the precious gift of salvation. He is seen ushering in our Lord and Savior to the world, as well as acknowledging the Father's pleasure of the Son. He is the *shofar* blowing, "Come see the King of kings! He is Emmanuel, God with us!"

2. Holy Spirit lives in us. It is devastating to know you have a precious gift, but have yet to open it. It is yours; you have access to it, but have not "received" it as if it is yours. Holy Spirit lives within us, and desires us to grow in greater capacities in God. It is like a shark put in an aquarium; it will only grow as large as it is able to fit inside of this enclosed space. If we are IN Christ, and have not accessed the power of Holy Spirit within, we will be confined in the box of religion and our growth is limited.

3. Holy Spirit seals believers. How many of us are looking for absolute guarantees in life? Well, nothing in life is guaranteed, but we can be confident that we are granted assurance of our salvation in Christ Jesus, but also the seal of Holy Spirit upon our lives. Holy Spirit is considered our "deposit" of eternal life!

4. Holy Spirit guides us. It is very frustrating driving and not knowing where you are going. Even having a GPS these days is questionable, because the signal cuts off from the satellite and can lead you in an entirely different direction that what you put in the device. Well, Holy Spirit is our spiritual GPS and we don't have to worry about any "satellite interference". He has direct access to the Creator of the Universe! Let Him guide you today!

5. Holy Spirit prompts us to worship. I am a worshipper! I love to bask in the presence of the Lord, whether it is in my home, my car, or corporately. Most worship is initiated by us when we feel like worshipping the Lord, but what happens when we are "prompted" by Holy Spirit to worship? I have been here and it is an unmistakable atmosphere of electrified worship to our King! It is not something that can be turned on or turned off; it is provoked by Him and it can only be finished by Him.

6. Holy Spirit empowers us for witness. When God does a unexplained work in us through Holy Spirit, it is inevitable that we desire to go out and share what He has done with others. When we allow Holy Spirit to have rule and reign in our hearts, we cannot contain, or restrain, what He desires to do within us. We are empowered to witness of the love of Jesus Christ and the power of His Spirit!

7. Holy Spirit enables us to understand and apply what is taught in the Word of God. How many times have you sat in a church service and not understood what the pastor was preaching? I have been in many churches all over the world for a span of almost forty years, from childhood to adulthood. It was not until I accessed the power of Holy Spirit within that the words began to "jump off the pages" to me; they now had LIFE! Holy Spirit inspired the writers of the Bible to pen His Words, so what better person to ignite their meaning to us than Him…Holy Spirit!

8. Holy Spirit will give life to our mortal bodies. This is a work of Holy Spirit that is yet to come. But the promise of that work is connected incredibly with the resurrection of Christ Himself: "If the Spirit of Him who raised Jesus from the dead is living in you, he who raised Christ from the dead will also give life to your mortal bodies through His Spirit, who lives in you." (Romans 8:11) If we pass on before the Second Coming of our Lord and Savior, Jesus Christ, rest assured that the same Breath of Life that raised Jesus from the dead will also raise us to eternal life with Him if we have, indeed, been born-again.

9. Holy Spirit transforms us in the sight of God. We cannot stay the same in God. Once we're born again, Holy Spirit takes up residence on the inside of us. His purpose is to lead us into a new life in Christ Jesus. Romans 12:2 says, "And be not conformed to this world, but be transformed by the renewing of your mind that you may prove what is that good and acceptable and perfect will of God." Holy Spirit is a huge part of our renewal process that leads to transformation.

10. Holy Spirit helps us to remember the Word of God. I don't know about you, but when I first began to study the Bible, I

51

couldn't remember a thing! I was really frustrated, until I actually acknowledged Holy Spirit as the guider He was assigned to be in my life. My knowledge and remembrance of Scripture grew rapidly after receiving Him into my life. John 14:26 says, "But the Helper, the Holy Spirit, whom the Father will send in My name, He will teach you all things, and bring to your remembrance all things that I said to you."

11. **Holy Spirit helps us to lead a godly life**. It is often difficult to discipline ourselves in any given task from what we eat to how we exercise. For some, it is their life's mission to be as healthy as they possibly can be. They put themselves on stringent diets and health regimens, and their second home is the gym. The Bible says, "For bodily exercise profits a little, but godliness is profitable for all things, having promise of the life that now is and of that which is to come." 1 Timothy 4:8

As we submit to the voice of Holy Spirit in our lives, He will instruct us on how to live the lives God has purposed for us. He leads us in the Truth by the Word of God and enables us to walk in total victory!

"But the fruit (evidence) of the Spirit is love, joy, peace, long-suffering, kindness, goodness, faithfulness, gentleness, self-control. Against such there is no law." Galatians 5:22-23, emphasis

12. **Holy Spirit gives us spiritual gifts for the edification of believers**. We all love to receive gifts, whether Birthday, Anniversary or Christmas; it is exciting to see what is underneath all that paper or hidden in that box. We know it is something that will make "us" happy or at least momentary happiness. But there are gifts God has purposed for us as His children that have nothing to do with our happiness, but for the edification, or uplifting, of another. These supernatural gifts are bestowed upon us by Holy Spirit.

"Even so you, since you are zealous for spiritual gifts, let it be for the edification of the church that you seek to excel." 1 Corinthians 14:12

"There are diversities of gifts, but the same Spirit. There are differences of ministries, but the same Lord. And there are diversities of activities, but it is the same God who works all in all. But the manifestation of the Spirit is given to each one for the profit of all:" 1 Corinthians 12:4-7

Let's take a look at the 9 spiritual gifts Holy Spirit imparts into the life of God's children:

❖ **Word of Wisdom**: Holy Spirit gives us the ability to accurately and properly apply the knowledge we have been given into a specific situation or circumstance.

❖ **Word of Knowledge**: Holy Spirit conveys insight, illumination or revelation to us that we would have otherwise had no knowledge concerning. Some call it foresight or foreknowledge.

❖ **The Gift of Faith**: Holy Spirit empowers a person, or increases their capacity, to receive faith on another level to do the Supernatural.

❖ **The Gift of Healing**: Holy Spirit manifests Himself through an individual full of faith to heal sicknesses and diseases, as well as empowers in deliverance.

❖ **Working of Miracles**: Holy Spirit endows an individual, or is *working through* an individual, to perform signs, wonders and miracles.

❖ **The Gift of Prophecy**: Holy Spirit transmits a direct Word from God to an individual to relay its message to another.

❖ **Discerning of Spirits**: Holy Spirit provides direct insight or oversight to an individual regarding specific spirits in operation within an individual, organization or region.

❖ **Different Kinds of Tongues**: Holy Spirit releases the ability within an individual to speak in different kinds of tongues, or languages, unknown to most for strategic intercession or purposes.

❖ **Interpretation of Tongues**: Holy Spirit opens up the eyes and ears of an individual's spirit to be able to decipher, or translate, what another person is speaking, praying or singing in the Spirit.

13. Holy Spirit is our guarantee of eternal life with God.

We don't have to guess, or assume, where we will reside in eternity. Through *Salvation, Justification, Adoption, Regeneration, Sanctification,* and ultimately *Glorification,* God has invested too much into our lives to leave us with the uncertainty of our eternal home. Holy Spirit gives us complete surety by sealing us with Himself! Let's just say He bets His entire existence upon us! We are sealed with the Promise of His Word! This is not like the world offers. The world will give us "Money Back Guarantees," but there is no need for us to return anything; we have the absolute GUARANTEE of eternal life with Father God and it is something you will never have to return! Oh, His Word is *settled in Heaven* concerning us! Glory to God!

"Now He who establishes us with you in Christ and has anointed us is God, who also has sealed us and given us the Spirit in our hearts as a guarantee." 2 Corinthians 1:21-22

"In Him you also trusted, after you heard the word of truth, the gospel of your salvation; in whom also, having believed, you were sealed with the Holy Spirit of promise, who is the guarantee of our inheritance until the redemption of the purchased possession, to the praise of His glory." Ephesians 1:13-14

The 7 Motivational Gifts of Holy Spirit:

"Having then gifts differing according to the grace that is given to us, let us use them: if prophecy, let us prophesy in proportion to our faith; or ministry, let us use it in our ministering; he who teaches, in teaching; he who exhorts, in exhortation; he who gives, with liberality; he who leads, with diligence; he who shows mercy, with cheerfulness." Romans 12:6-8

- **Prophecy**: A person with the motivational gift of prophecy applies the Word of God to a situation so that sin is exposed and relationships are restored. He or she has a strong sense of right and wrong and speaks out against compromise and evil.

- **Ministry (Serving)**: A person with the motivational gift of serving is driven to demonstrate love by meeting practical needs. The server is available to see a project through to the end and enjoys doing physical work.

- **Teacher**: A person with the motivational gift of teaching is passionate about discovering and validating truth. A teacher is particularly concerned with the accuracy of information, especially church doctrine, and is often gifted with research abilities.

- **Exhorting**: A person with the motivational gift of exhortation wants to see believers grow to spiritual maturity. An exhorter is an encourager at heart and is often involved in the ministries of counseling, teaching, and training disciples.

- **Giving**: A person with the motivational gift of giving wants to use financial resources wisely in order to give to meet the needs of others. A giver is usually good at finding the best buy, noticing overlooked needs, and maintaining a budget.

- **Leader (Administration/Organizer)**: A person with the motivational gift of organizing is able to accomplish tasks and solve problems through analysis and delegation. An organizer often discerns the talents and abilities of others and knows how those individuals can best serve within a ministry or on a particular project.

- **Mercy**: A person with the motivational gift of mercy is sensitive to the emotional and spiritual needs of others. A mercy-giver is drawn to people in need and seeks to demonstrate compassion, understanding, and love to them.

So again, we see Holy Spirit's fingerprint on many of the functionalities within the lives of God's people, both for spiritual and motivational edification. If you desire to know and understand your purpose in life, get to know the purpose of *Holy Spirit*. He is directly connected to your destiny!

Mother Teresa

"Christ prays in me, Christ works in me, Christ thinks in me, Christ looks through my eyes, Christ speaks through my words, Christ works with my hands, Christ walks with my feet, Christ loves with my heart. As St Paul's prayer was: "I belong to Christ and nothing will separate me from the love of Christ." It was that oneness, oneness with God in the Holy Spirit."

"All of us are but His instruments who do our part and pass by."
~Mother Teresa

Chapter 4
The Position of Holy Spirit

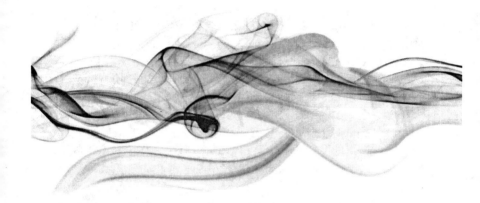

"Grace to you and peace from Him who is and who was and who is to come, and from the seven Spirits who are before His throne, and from Jesus Christ, the faithful witness, the firstborn from the dead, and the ruler over the kings of the earth." Revelation 1: 4b-6

It is important to recognize that position is absolutely pertinent for strategy. When something or someone is out place, or position, it can directly or indirectly affect many other situations and/or people. It is not only important to be in position, but also to know the "*who, what, when, how and where*" to operate from that position. This is all possible with the aid of Holy Spirit. In His infinite wisdom and intelligence, He relays the mind of God as it relates to our lives in each season. So, it is crucial that we are able to hear and discern the thoughts, intents and mind of Holy Spirit.

Discernment is the ability to judge well. In Biblical context, it is perception in the absence of judgment with a view to obtaining spiritual direction and understanding. This means to gain the purest form of God's heart and mind in a situation that we can successfully make decisions according to His perfect will. One of the most frustrating things in life is to think we can see clearly, when in reality, we are the furthest from God's heart in a matter. As we continue to meditate upon the Word of God and remain led by Holy Spirit, our spiritual *discernment* will be accurate. God desires for His people to be in strategic position to hear from Him in every situation and in every season of their lives. Seek Holy Spirit fervently for spiritual *discernment*. If you remember nothing else from this book, remember this... "Holy Spirit will NEVER contradict the Word of God!" His ultimate position is to confirm, not contradict, God's Holy Word, because He inspired it!

Confirmation in Catholicism is one of the seven sacraments through which Catholics pass in the process of their religious upbringing. According to Catholic doctrine, in this sacrament, they are sealed with the Gift of the Holy Spirit and are strengthened in their Christian life. One thing I admire greatly concerning the Catholic Church is the understanding of the need for God's Spirit in our lives. Though we recognize, as born-again believers, Holy Spirit is immediately activated into our lives, the sad reality is that many of us neglect His presence. Catholics usually initiate this sacrament around the age of twelve or thirteen. Aren't you glad we don't have to wait to receive the precious gift of Holy Spirit in a ceremony? He is ready and waiting for us to receive Jesus Christ as our Lord and to begin His assignment in our lives.

Though this *Confirmation* is more of a religious act, let's delve deeper into the spirit of the word *confirmation*. According to Merriam-Webster's definition, confirmation is the proof which shows that something is true or correct, or the process of supporting a statement by evidence. The word *confirm* is the Greek word *bebaioó*, which means confirm, ratify, establish, to pass or guarantee. It also means properly, to walk where it is solid, (reliable, guaranteed); hence, make sure, or fully reliable. This is what happens when Holy Spirit speaks to us. Holy Spirit will confirm many things in our lives, as we submit to His voice.

In *The Four Positions of the Holy Spirit,*[iii] author Charles Morris reveals the strategic positions of Holy Spirit within our lives and what each of them represents. Here are the four positions:

❖ The Holy Spirit, a divine personality, comes along BESIDE US, convicting us and wooing us to the heart of the Father.

❖ Once we are born again, the Holy Spirit moves WITHIN US, revealing the character of the Father to us and through us.

❖ When we are baptized with the Holy Spirit, He comes UPON US, imbuing us with power to be a bold witness in these last days.

❖ As we surrender daily to the leadership of the person of the Holy Spirit, He FILLS US with His presence and leads us in His will and ways.

Holy Spirit has so many different roles He plays not only in our individual lives, but also in the course of this earthly realm, as well as the Heavenly. He stands unmovable and unshakable in His assignment and will accomplish all God has commissioned Him to do and be in the course of this world. There are other significant positions we need to look at in order to grasp the fullness of Holy Spirit's work in the earth.

1. **Holy Spirit is eternal in His nature**.
    "...how much more shall the blood of Christ, who through the eternal Spirit offered Himself without spot to God,

59

cleanse your conscience from dead works to serve the living God?" (Hebrews 9:14)

The word *eternal* means lasting or existing forever; without end or beginning. The Greek word for eternal is *aiónios*, which means age-long, and therefore: practically eternal, unending; partaking of the character of that which lasts for an age, as contrasted with that which is brief and fleeting.

He was in the Beginning, He is in the End and He is everywhere in between. His existence spans eternity: past, present and future. What a revelation of His faithfulness!

2. **Holy Spirit is Omnipresent**.
   "Where can I go from Your Spirit? Or where can I flee from Your presence? If I ascend into heaven, You are there; If I make my bed in hell, behold, You are there. If I take the wings of morning, And dwell in the uttermost parts of the sea, Even there Your hand shall lead me, And Your right hand shall hold me." (Psalm 139:7-10)

Omnipresent means all-present. This term means that God is capable of being everywhere at the same time. It means His divine presence, Holy Spirit, encompasses the whole of the universe. Isn't it comforting to know that out of the 7.4 billion people on the earth today, we don't have to wait in line to talk to Holy Spirit personally? We have the assurance that He is so all encompassing that He is able to individually help all that call upon the name of Jesus Christ and receive Him to fulfill their purpose in this life.

3. **Holy Spirit is Omnipotent**.
   "All the inhabitants of the earth are accounted as nothing, But He does according to His will in the host of heaven And among the inhabitants of earth; And no one can ward off His hand or say to Him, 'What have You done?'" (Daniel 4:35)

Omnipotent means (of a deity) having unlimited power; able to do anything. God is considered the Omnipotent One. His name is *El Shaddai,* which means "self-sufficient," "all-sufficient," or "almighty." God's power is unlimited. His Spirit, Holy Spirit, has full access to God's heavenly arsenal at His disposal.

"Since He has at His command all the power in the universe, the Lord God omnipotent can do anything as easily as anything else. All His acts are done without effort. He expends no energy that must be replenished. His self-sufficiency makes it unnecessary for Him to look outside of Himself for a renewal of strength. All the power required to do all that He wills to do lies in undiminished fullness in His own infinite being."[iv] A.W. Tozer

4. **Holy Spirit is Omniscient.**
   "But God has revealed them to us through His Spirit. For the Spirit searches all things, yes, the deep things of God. For what man knows the things of a man except the spirit of the man which is in him? Even so no one knows the things of God except the Spirit of God." (1 Corinthians 2:10, 11)

Omniscient means knowing everything. It is "the state of having total knowledge, the quality of knowing everything." For God to be sovereign over His creation of all things, whether visible or invisible, He has to be all-knowing. His omniscience is not restricted to any one person in the Godhead—Father, Son, and Holy Spirit are all by nature *omniscient.*

It is encouraging to know that our Father knows everything. The Bible says even when we don't know what to pray, the Spirit, Holy Spirit, prays through us and we can be assured that He prays according to the Will of God for our lives. He knows what we need when we do not. We can rest in knowing there is a team that is fighting for us in the heavenly realm.

We saw Holy Spirit's role in relation to the Creation of the Universe. "By the word of the Lord were the heavens made; and all the host of them by the breath (Spirit) of his mouth," (Psalm 33:6). Job 33:4 reveals Holy Spirit's hand in the Creation of man: "The Spirit of God hath made me, and the breath of the Almighty hath given me life." His power is seen also in the preservation of nature. "The grass withers, the flower fades, because the breath of the Lord blows upon it…" Isaiah 40:7

We also saw His presence all over Jesus Christ at His birth, life, death and resurrection, but now let us look at His position in the impartation of God's Holy Word.

- **Holy Spirit is the Author of the Scriptures**. The Scriptures came by the inbreathing of God; the Breath of Life, Holy Spirit.

"Knowing this first, that no prophecy of Scripture is of any private interpretation, for prophecy never came by the will of man, but holy men of God spoke as they were moved by the Holy Spirit." (2 Peter 1:20-21)

We assume the ministry of Holy Spirit is only New Testament theology, but we have a plethora of Old Testament scripture that reveals the *Omnipotent, Omnipresent* and *Omniscient* Spirit of God speaking from Genesis to Revelation. From Moses to John, and all the prophets in between, these men of God were inspired by Holy Spirit to write what they heard from Him. And this inspiration did not cease with the writers of The Holy Bible, but has traveled throughout the generations to those that have submitted their hearts, minds and yes, ears to the heartbeat of Father God, Holy Spirit. I am a living witness of this "scribal anointing". As I read back over the books I have written, I know without a shadow of a doubt that it had to be Holy Spirit leading my pen, because I could never, in and of myself, write in such a manner. The words of those pages "speak" to me to this day, and have come alive in ways unimaginable. The books of many others that communicated the heart of God through inspiration of Holy Spirit are life transforming messages. Many of these authors I have followed for years and they have helped me learn to hear the voice of God in my own life. They are Spirit and they are life, just as the Word of God is to us today. He hasn't changed His position. He is the same yesterday, today and forevermore!

"All Scripture is given by inspiration of God, and is profitable for doctrine, for reproof, for correction, for instruction in righteousness," (2 Timothy 3:16)

The Holy Bible is our lifeline. It is our earthly manual dedicated to instructing us to live the lives God intended for us. Its wisdom is limitless, and Holy Spirit inspires us, as He hears from Father God.

- **Holy Spirit is the Interpreter of the Scriptures.** Holy Spirit possesses the heart and mind of Father God. He is able to clearly and articulately release God's intent and motive for humanity through the Word of God.

"He will glorify Me, for He will take of what is Mine and declare it to you. All things that the Father has are Mine. Therefore I said that He will take of Mine and declare it to you." (John 16:14-15)

Now, let's study the work of Holy Spirit within the lives of Believers.

1. **Holy Spirit Empowers the Believer for Life and Service.** "For the law of the Spirit of life in Christ Jesus hath made me free from the law of sin and death." (Romans 8:2)

There are two natures in the believer: the flesh and the Spirit. "For the flesh lusts against the Spirit and the Spirit against the flesh; and these are contrary to one another, so that you do not do

63

the things that you wish." (Galatians 5:17) Holy Spirit enables the believer to reign over sin through His Spirit within. Holy Spirit in the heart of a Believer is the secret of victory over sin.

Holy Spirit also produces the blessed fruit of the Christian life. "But the fruit of the Spirit is love, joy, peace, longsuffering, kindness, goodness, faithfulness, gentleness, self-control. Against such there is no law." (Galatians 5:22-23) Holy Spirit stands in the *stead* of Father God. Everything He is, He desires us to be. The works of the flesh are polar opposite of the Fruit of the Spirit. "Now the works of the flesh are evident, which are: adultery, fornication, uncleanness, lewdness, idolatry, sorcery, hatred, contentions, jealousies, outbursts of wrath, selfish ambitions, dissensions, heresies, envy, murders, drunkenness, revelries, and the like; of which I tell you beforehand, just as I also told you in time past, that those who practice such things will not inherit the kingdom of God." (Galatians 5:19-21) The fruit of the Spirit can be categorized into three groups: the first, in relation to God: love, joy, and peace; the second, in relation to our fellow man: longsuffering, gentleness, and goodness; and the third, for our individual Christian life: faith, meekness, and self-control.

The thought that He is able to keep us from fulfilling the lusts of the flesh is astounding! "I say then: Walk in the Spirit, and you shall not fulfill the lust of the flesh." (Galatians 5:16) As we stay close in His presence, He will totally transform our lives.

2. Holy Spirit is the Guide of the Believer's Life.
Holy Spirit guides every single step of our lives if we allow Him. When we accept Jesus Christ as our Lord, we also accept Holy Spirit as our Guide through this new life in Christ. "For as many as are led by the Spirit of God, these are sons of God." (Romans 8:14)

He is able to lead and guide us through the most turbulent of seasons and right into the perfect will of God for our lives. In fact,

His position is to walk *with* us, many times, in front of us, so we are not bombarded by the enemy. He knows what is ahead, and will warn us if we would just heed His guidance.

So many lives throughout Scripture were under the direct guidance of Holy Spirit.

3. Holy Spirit Anoints the Believer.

"But the anointing which you have received from Him abides in you, and you do not need that anyone teach you; but as the same anointing teaches you concerning all things, and is true, and is not a lie, and just as it has taught you, you will abide in Him." (1 John 2:27)

This anointing provides *knowledge and teaching*. As Holy Spirit abides in the life of a Believer, supernatural knowledge and wisdom is imparted. We are blessed with pastors and teachers to administer the Word of God into our lives, but more importantly, we should be searching the scriptures daily for ourselves and hearing what God is saying to us directly. The written Word is considered the *logos* of scripture, but when we hear directly from Holy Spirit, is considered *rhema*, or the inner voice of the Spirit. He speaks directly to each and every one of us individually. He is able to teach us all we need to know to walk in victory in Christ Jesus. What person is able to do such things?

"But you have an anointing from the Holy One, and you know all things." 1 John 2:20

Holy Spirit also anoints for *service*. "The Spirit of the Lord is upon Me, because He has anointed Me to preach the gospel to the poor; He has sent Me to heal the brokenhearted, to proclaim liberty to the captives and recovery of sight to the blind, to set at liberty those who are oppressed;" Luke 4:18

65

There is much we cannot do in our own power. We need the supernatural endowment of Holy Spirit to carry out our earthly assignments. The anointing, or the Anointed One, is Christ Himself within us, through Holy Spirit, carrying out God's perfect will in the earth realm.

Finally, Holy Spirit anoints for *consecration.* In the Old Testament, the prophets, priests and kings were anointed for consecration. *Consecration* is the solemn dedication to a special purpose or service, usually religious in nature. In Biblical context, it is considered the separation of oneself from things that are unclean, especially anything that would contaminate one's relationship with a perfect God. *Consecration* also carries the connotation of sanctification, holiness, or purity.

The importance of being consecrated, or pure, in our relationship with God is emphasized in the book of Joshua. After forty years in the wilderness, the children of Israel were about to cross over the Jordan River into the Promised Land. They were then given a command and a promise: "Joshua told the people, 'Consecrate yourselves, for tomorrow the LORD will do amazing things among you.'" (Joshua 3:5)

Many of us desire to do great things for God, but are not willing to *consecrate*, or set ourselves apart, from the world to truly be used by Him. We must understand that we cannot mix the holy with the profane. God will not anoint us, neither consecrate us, if we refuse to crucify our flesh and walk in the Spirit. Too many today believe they are anointed, or believe God has placed His anointing upon them, but He is nowhere to be found. Pride, arrogance, greed and rebellion will cause the Lord to lift His hand from upon our lives, especially if we are in a position of speaking into the lives of His people. He will not be named among such foolishness and upheaval.

All throughout the ages, Holy Spirit is seen in the execution of God's promises for the earth and His children. He is the culmination between promise and fulfillment. He is the bridge connecting the earthly and heavenly. He is the conduit through which Father God communes with His Creation. There is no greater gift in the earth realm than that of *Holy Spirit*. God loves us so very much!

A.W. Tozer

"If the Holy Spirit was withdrawn from the church today, 95 percent of what we do would go on and no one would know the difference. If the Holy Spirit had been withdrawn from the New Testament church, 95 percent of what they did would stop, and everybody would know the difference."

"The Spirit-filled life is not a special, deluxe edition of Christianity. It is part and parcel of the total plan of God for His people."
~*A.W. Tozer*

Chapter 5

The Power of Holy Spirit

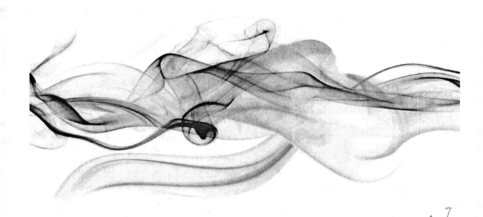

"But you shall receive power when the Holy Spirit has come upon you; and you shall be witnesses to Me in Jerusalem, and in all Judea and Samaria, and to the end of the earth." Acts 1:8

Before I received Holy Spirit into my life, truly acknowledged His presence at work in and through me, I was an immature follower of Christ. I loved the Lord immensely, yet I did not have the power of God at work in my life. I went to church every Sunday and every Wednesday, as well as several times throughout the week for classes and ministry work. I served faithfully in God's house and loved God and His people with all of my heart, but something was missing. I was a praying woman, but I lacked the power of God to hit the target in prayer. There are several words I want to acknowledge in regards to God's power. The first one we will discuss is the word *dunamis.*

Dunamis is the Greek word for power. It is defined as (miraculous) power, might and strength. It also means the ability to perform, or power to achieve, by applying the Lord's inherent abilities. The word *dunamis* is used over 120 times in the New Testament.

"And do not lead us into temptation, But deliver us from the evil one. For Yours is the kingdom and the power *(dunamis)* and the glory forever. Amen. Matthew 6:13, emphasis

As Believers in Jesus Christ, we must understand that we have been given power *(dunamis)* by God to carry out His perfect will in the earth realm. This is not a power that comes through natural strength or ability, but we are endowed, or equipped, by the Lord Himself, through the *conduit* of Holy Spirit. The word *conduit* means a natural or artificial channel through which something (as a fluid) is conveyed. We also recognize this word in dealing with electricity as the means through which it flows back and forth through a conductor. *Conduits* in the Bible were channels that allowed for the disbursement of water sources to supply the Temple in Jerusalem with free-flowing, unhindered water, also called aqueducts. If these *conduits*, or channels, were blocked, the people would eventually have no running source of water, as well as the Temple. Holy Spirit is the *conduit* of God for our lives. He is the source through which God speaks to His people. Without the words of life spoken through Holy Spirit, we are a people left to the sin, and ultimate destruction, of our souls. He gives us the power to overcome sin through the Word of God; to be transformed by the renewing of our minds. He is at work *within* us enabling us to walk by the Spirit and not by the lusts of the flesh.

God speaks to His people Holy Spirit

Holy Spirit free-flowing unhindered can be hindered

Teaving sheep open to wolves,

The Power of Holy Spirit

As I said before, He is available to us, but until we acknowledge Him in our lives, this power, or *dunamis*, is left dormant, unavailable to us, God's people. God always uses a "vessel," or *conduit*, through which to accomplish His plans in the earth. He sent His only Son, Jesus Christ, to redeem the world of sin. His birth, life, death, burial and resurrection provided our salvation and He took the sin of the world upon Himself. Through Holy Spirit, God seals that salvation and places us on the journey toward becoming more and more like Him every day. Now we, as followers of Christ, are to be the *conduit* of God's love and mercy toward humanity. Christians are the *conduit* through which the grace of God flows to others. We have to be connected if we are going to be vessels of God's grace. Our ability to bear fruit is contingent on being connected to Christ, the Vine, and led by His Spirit.

"Abide in Me, and I in you. As the branch cannot bear fruit of itself, unless it abides in the vine, neither can you, unless you abide in Me." John 15:4

Much of the Church today is in total chaos and confusion, because of the lack of the most important gift imparted to her, and that is Holy Spirit. It is evident that in most churches across the world, there is no surrendering to or leading of Holy Spirit. Man has taken it upon himself to be the head of the Church, instead of Jesus Christ. Instead of prayer, fasting and laboring in the Word of God, most pastors today are booking their itineraries to capacity all over the world and leaving the sheep open to wolves. They are putting together three to five conferences a year at their church and hiring marketing, advertising and PR firms to promote these conferences to the masses and to bring in the most influential pastors, singers and musicians from around the world to "speak a word" to their congregants. God has given *you* His Word for His people and entrusted *you* with the teaching, training and equipping of His children. How in the world can they hear clearly when multiple voices and visions are being dumped upon them all throughout the year? I submit to you that this is neither God nor

71

His Spirit. It is the pride and greed of man and the spirit of *Mammon* in operation, period.

When we are not led by Holy Spirit, there is no power (*Dunamis*) available. We forfeit the presence of God when we choose to be the thermostat of the Church, cutting off the "spirit" when and how we decide. We plan our services with extravagant lights, celebrity singers, and eloquent orators that summon the praise and glory of the people, instead of leading them to the One who shares His glory with no one! These services are riddled with entertainment and showmanship. They will "conjure" up what they call Holy Spirit and the anointing of God, but I am here to declare to you that Holy Spirit is not a ghost or a witch you can just conjure up in the spirit when you need Him and shut Him off at your leisure! He is God! He is fully God and fully Spirit, on assignment in the earth realm. It sickens me when I see the foolery acted out in many churches around the world. Holy Spirit is nowhere to be found in some of these "circus tents". Yet, they will swear up and down of healings, deliverance and salvation. These are shows to display these false teachers and prophets and their fame. They manipulate and deceive people through emotional psychosis and try to put God's name upon it, all for the "miraculous" offering that will come thereafter. I am not merely vomiting this message out to you. I have lived this. I have witnessed it with my own eyes, as I have been in leadership in several of these kinds of churches.

I would sit, many times, with tears rolling down my face wondering how in the world some of these pastors could call what they were doing Spirit-led. I would weep during these services, as I saw the glory and adoration being extended toward a man, instead of God. As Worship was proceeding, entourages of pastors and their security would be paraded in the side door of the stage, and led in front of the congregation to their "VIP" seats, with thousand dollar suits, dresses, flashy jewelry, handbags and stilettos on all for the "fans" to see and take pictures of them. Yes, during Worship

Man lifting up man

and yes, people not concerned about worshipping the Lord, but what the pastor, or speaker, is wearing. "Selfies" being taken and flashes all over the church. The roaring applause as a pastor's bio was being read like they were announcing a WWF wrestling match? As the pastor approached the pulpit, masses of people would jump to their feet and scream out his/her name with camera flashes everywhere? I felt as if I was in a rock concert or on the red carpet at a Hollywood premier, which of course, red carpets were lining the front entrances of these church conferences. I felt as if I was the only one not standing to applaud these pastors/speakers. I would close my eyes and just intercede that God would come in, regardless of this idol worship, and touch the people that needed a touch from Heaven.

As the "show" began, people were already up on their feet and all the speaker had to do was breathe heavy or shout and everyone was shouting along with them? There is rarely a mention of the name of Jesus, but most "sermons" today are about personal affirmation, wealth building or attacking your *haters*? There is *no power (Dunamis)* being released, because it does not stem from man, but God! There is power in the name of Jesus! The Bible says in Philippians 2:9-12:

> "Therefore God also has highly exalted Him and given Him the name which is above every name, that at the name of Jesus every knee should bow, of those in heaven, and of those on earth, and of those under the earth, and that every tongue should confess that Jesus Christ is Lord, to the glory of God the Father."

We have to understand that the power of God, through Holy Spirit, is the only way we can do anything on this earth in His name. We have no power outside of the *dunamis* of God. Let's look at several other scriptures that reveal the power of God:

e angel answered and said to her, "The Holy Spirit will
ae upon you, and the power of the Most High will overshadow you; and for that reason the holy Child shall be called
the Son of God." Luke 1:35

"And Jesus returned to Galilee in the power of the Spirit, and
news about Him spread through all the surrounding district."
Luke 4:14

"And behold, I am sending forth the promise of My Father
upon you; but you are to stay in the city until you are clothed
with power from on high." Luke 24:49

According to a Charisma Magazine article by J. Lee Grady[v], he
shares six reasons, or blockages, for a Believer not receiving the
fullness of the power of God through Holy Spirit:

1. Doubt or intellectual pride
2. Religious tradition
3. Fear of the supernatural
4. Unconfessed sin
5. Emotional wounds
6. An unyielded spirit

I can easily add several other reasons, but just refer back a few
paragraphs and it will be easily recognizable. If we desire the
fullness of God's power operating within us, we need to address
these issues in our spiritual lives. Many Believers can identify with
one or more, or even all, of these "blockages". There is nothing
more devastating on earth than a powerless Believer in Jesus
Christ. Our witness is affected not only by the refusal to share the
Gospel of Jesus Christ, but also trying to offer it without the
dunamis power of God through Holy Spirit. It is clear from Acts 1:8
that it is in *His* power only that we are even able to witness Jesus to
the world. If we deny Holy Spirit, how do we think we are able to
effectively share Jesus with the world? We are professionals in

inviting people to Church, but how much power do we have
to bring them to the throne room of grace, to the feet of Jesus
Christ, to become a born-again Believer? I think this is something
we really need to ponder upon.

The next word I want to discuss in relation to Holy Spirit
power is *Exousia*. The definition of *Exousia* is the power to act,
authority. It also means conferred power, delegated empowerment,
or operating in a designated jurisdiction. *Exousia* is the authority
given to us *from* God, *by* the redeemed blood of Jesus Christ, and
through the vein of Holy Spirit. Just as we are unable to effectively
witness the Gospel without the *dunamis*, power of God, we also
cannot express it without the *Exousia*, or authority, in Christ Jesus.
If we don't know who we are in Christ, how can we offer Him to
someone else?

"...Christ IN us, the hope of glory." Colossians 1:27, emphasis

It is in this power (*dunamis*) and authority (*Exousia*) that Holy
Spirit moves through the Believer to effectively reach this world
with the love of Jesus Christ.

"But that you may know that the Son of Man has power
(Exousia) on earth to forgive sins"—then He said to the para-
lytic, "Arise, take up your bed, and go to your house." Matthew
9:6

The same power and authority Jesus had to forgive sins and
heal the sick here on earth has been extended to us, His followers.
In fact, He says that we would do greater works than He did. (John
14:12) To have the same power, and even greater, as Jesus Christ,
available to me is unfathomable? The same power that lifted Him
out of the clutches of the grave? The same power that raised
Lazarus from the dead? Yes, it is absolutely available to us today if
we have surrendered our lives to the Lord Jesus Christ and the
leading of Holy Spirit.

"And when He had called His twelve disciples to Him, He gave them *power* over unclean spirits, to cast them out, and to heal all kinds of sickness and all kinds of disease." Matthew 10:1, emphasis

The *Exousia*, or authority, of God given to us, His disciples, in the earth realm is really one of our greatest assignments as born-again Believers. He is giving us *HIS* authority! He is providing us with the supernatural ability to carry out His will on earth; just as it is in Heaven. (Matthew 6:10) There are so many hurting, depressed, sick and diseased people in this dark world. So many are in utter darkness, yet *WE*, the people of God, have the answer for them, not only in Jesus Christ for their souls to be saved and to live eternally with Him, but also here in the earth. The power and authority we possess is far beyond what many of us understand. It is sad to know that the one entity with the greatest authority in the earth realm does not operate in it, the Church. We have the power *by* God Himself, *in* Christ Jesus, and *through* Holy Spirit to lay hands on the sick and they will recover; to cast out demons and heal all manner of sickness and disease. I not only believe this to be in the physical sense, but also emotionally, mentally and spiritually. To see so many spiritually bound people in this world, even in the Church, is absolutely devastating to me. What is missing from the lives of those that claim to follow Jesus Christ...*Holy Spirit!* Not accessing the power of God within is like going into a battle deaf and blind.

Why are we not seeing the modern day Church operating in the full power and authority of God? There are many reasons, but one of the major reasons is because we have erected idols in our lives and in our churches. God will share His glory with no man. When we have made a choice to idolize our spiritual leaders, we then erect altars of worship to man, instead of God. His supernatural power and presence is cut off from His people and we stand in the "place" of God. I don't care how many *prayers* you offer up, or how many times you *lay your hands* upon someone to be healed, delivered or set free; it will not happen without the power and presence of

Almighty God through Holy Spirit. We quench the Spirit of God when we arrogantly and ignorantly try to do any of this in our own, limited, power. The word *quench* means to extinguish, put out, snuff out, smother or douse, as with fire. The Greek word for quench is *shennumi*, which means to extinguish or suppress. We have literally suppressed the Spirit of God in our lives, as well as our places of Worship, because of pride and greed. We want to get the glory for *raising* the dead, for *healing* the sick and diseased, for *casting out* demons, for *delivering* people from bondage, for *opening* blind eyes and deaf ears, for *feeding* the poor, for *counseling* the nations, for *growing* the Church and why not, let's go here...for *saving* people's souls! Why am I emphasizing these things and going to this extent to speak in this manner? Because when we try to do these things in our own power and for our own glory, without God and without the sacrifice of His Son, Jesus Christ and the power of Holy Spirit, we are operating in pure deceit, manipulation and ultimately, witchcraft!

All too often, we see this happening in the Church today. Any pastor or spiritual leader that denies Holy Spirit but claims to lay hands on people for healing or for ordination is deceived! Laying hands on Believers is an act, or endowment, of Holy Spirit. Just as we discussed the anointing oil earlier; it is a symbol of Holy Spirit and when used in the laying on of hands for any purpose, it is merely a point of contact for someone's faith. So it baffles me when so many try to leave Holy Spirit out of His assignment in our lives? In essence, we are *quenching* the Spirit of God for our own personal fame, as well as gain. I truly want to encourage the Body of Christ here. If you are in need of healing or deliverance of any sort, whether physical, emotional, mental or spiritual, DO NOT believe that you have to give money to receive what is freely available to you by faith! There are so many false teachers and false prophets in the world today that are deceiving people into believing that as you "sow a seed," God will heal or deliver you. The devil is a liar! It is by the power of Holy Spirit that God is able to touch the lives of His precious children in the earth realm.

"Do not quench the Spirit." 1 Thessalonians 5:19

I am not sure many people understand fully that they are, indeed, *quenching* the Spirit of God, Holy Spirit. Let's look at nine ways in which we can quench the Spirit of God:

- ❖ We ignore the leading that we know is Holy Spirit.
- ❖ We purposefully disobey God's Word.
- ❖ We become so self–reliant that we no longer need God.
- ❖ We think grace will get us out of everything.
- ❖ We allow pride to rob us when we know God is calling us to humility.
- ❖ We teach people that God isn't speaking to us anymore.
- ❖ We are more concerned with being liked by man than being approved by God.
- ❖ We put off what God is saying now, expecting to do it later in life.
- ❖ We structure church services to the point that the program is more important that the leading of Holy Spirit.

"How little chance the Holy Spirit has nowadays. The churches and missionary societies have so bound Him in red tape that they practically ask Him to sit in a corner while they do the work themselves."[vi] C.T. Studd

Wow! What a devastating reality.

We are not only shortchanging ourselves, but the people of God from experiencing the true, authentic power of the living God, *Holy Spirit*. Why would spiritual leaders do such things? Sad to say, not much has changed since the early Church. Power, prestige, fame, money and glory has so engulfed the Church that if we release the full power and authority of God, through the power of Holy Spirit, there is no more profit for the "moneychangers". People are held in bondage by the very establishment that is supposed to be the conduit of freedom in the earth, the Church. I am thoroughly convinced that millions of people around the world have been held back from healing, deliverance, and yes, true salvation, because of the selfishness and greed of many of our spiritual leaders and organizations. By the withholding of the fullness of God through Holy Spirit, the Church remains in spiritual bondage.

I have sat in church services where there is a "masquerading" of Holy Spirit. Mocked healing and deliverance was evident to the one able to discern by the Spirit of God. Just because a pastor says, "I feel the anointing" or "I hear you Holy Spirit" does not mean that He is present or speaking. Immature believers in Christ Jesus flock to churches, seminars and conferences seeking for man to lay hands on them or to speak a word of prophecy to them. They seek signs and wonders, instead of seeking the One that is able to free them from the chains of bondage, and these pastors feed off of their spiritual ignorance. I have witnessed so much chaos and confusion over my saved life. I have seen people come up to get "healed" or "delivered" just to get close to the pastor or to be seen on television. As I stated before, those that are able to discern know when something is *of the Spirit* and when it is "flesh". One of my deepest concerns is pastors that allow this when they know it is deception. A pastor, or a shepherd, should have the greatest discernment in a church. We should only be laying hands on people as *led* by Holy Spirit.

"Do not lay hands on anyone hastily, nor share in other people's sins; keep yourself pure." 1 Timothy 5:22

This is an epidemic in most churches today. There is more foolishness taking place than the preached Word of God. Holy Spirit is not a "circus act". We should never come into a church expecting Holy Spirit to show up and entertain us. He comes to confirm the Word of God. If we taught the Word of God line upon line, precept upon precept, much of this manipulation and deception would not be taking place. The Spirit of God will *always* line up with the Word of God. They will *never* contradict one another. The Word of God and Holy Spirit work together in unison and therefore spiritual order is completely established. When one or the other is not established, chaos and confusion will inevitably ensue and spiritual abuse is more likely to transpire.

The sad reality is that the Pentecostalism movement and the other "overly spiritualized" sects of Christianity have done more damage to the Church than any other denomination that outright denies the existence of Holy Spirit. It's one thing to deny Him, but to deceive people through emotionalism and sensationalism is outright manipulation. Shouting, screaming, running through the church, and jumping up and down, aggressive laying on of hands where people fall over one another, on the floor and on chairs is mostly for show, instead of the leading and prompting of Holy Spirit. People have been so accustomed to this kind of church service that if it does not happen at least once in a service, then they feel God has not met them there. Most born-again Believers in Jesus Christ within these denominations and movements cannot sit through a preached sermon without shouting or "interrupting" the Word of God. They are, in actuality, immature in the things of the Spirit. I, too, was one of these people. I have been in churches all over the world, and have been taught many different ways and experienced many different ways in prayer, worship, healing, deliverance and much more. It was not until I began to truly seek the leading of Holy Spirit for myself through the Word of God that I began to understand who He was and who He was not; how He moves and how He does not; how He speaks and how He does not. I had to "unlearn" a lot and had to discipline myself by His leading.

Theatrics is not a sign of Holy Spirit. In fact, more often than not, it is a sign of our flesh, as well as the prompting of the enemy. We would rather be entertained than sit and hear what God is saying to us through Holy Spirit. And we can be assured that the enemy does not want us to hear what God is speaking for our lives, so he encourages confusion at every level. I remember one Sunday after service, I was speaking with some dear friends just catching up and there was some chaos going on in the corner of the sanctuary. We looked over and there was a group of elders encircling a woman that just kept screaming. I knew they were trying to "cast a demon" out of her, but it was just taking way too long. We stood there for almost thirty minutes watching these elders back and forth, one after another, aggressively screaming for this demon to come out. I knew, for one, that this many people had no business being over there. It doesn't take that many people to cast out a demon. Secondly, after nothing seemed to be working, a pastor walked across the platform boldly as if he was about to go and show these elders how it is done. He, too, *played* with this spirit and the woman actually walked away from them all close to where we were on the other side of the altar. She caught eye contact with me and when I tell you the smirk on this woman's face let me know she knew not one of these elders, or even the pastor, had the power or authority to cast it out. I recognized her from when I first came to this church. I remember standing after one service watching a couple who were pastors walk over and remove a couple who were elders that were trying to cast the demon out of her. They were not able to and neither were these pastors. Again, over thirty minutes passed and me, having no authority in this church, though I knew I had the authority in the Spirit, stood and watched helplessly for this bound woman.

I have witnessed these things more often than I'd like to admit. To stand at an altar and to be able to "see" spirits, demons, in and on people and then to see leaders in the church just putting on a show so others will see and hear their eloquent prayers grieved me deeply. I would see these people walk up bound, and watch them walk away even more bound; no healing and no deliverance. This takes place more often than not in today's church. Another reason we are not seeing true, authentic healing and deliverance is because of sin, not in the lives of the oppressed coming to be set free, but in the lives of those laying hands and praying for healing and deliverance. The Word of God says that sin separates us from the Lord.

> "But your iniquities have separated you from your God; And your sins have hidden His face from you, So that He will not hear." Isaiah 59:2

We have got to repent and turn back to the Lord. So many of God's people are in darkness and bondage, yet we call ourselves followers of Jesus Christ. How can we effectively win this world to Christ if we, the children of Light, are in just as much darkness, if not more, than the world?

It is time to set the people of God free!

> "But if the Spirit of Him who raised Jesus from the dead dwells in you, He who raised Christ from the dead will also give life to your mortal bodies through His Spirit who dwells in you." Romans 8:11

> "and what is the exceeding greatness of His *power* toward us who believe, according to the working of His mighty *power* which He worked in Christ when He raised Him from the dead and seated Him at His right hand in the heavenly places, far above all principality and power and might and dominion, and every name that is named, not only in this age but also in that which is to come." Ephesians 1:19-21, emphasis

Holy Spirit empowers us to be witnesses for our Lord Jesus Christ.

> "And with great power the apostles gave witness to the resurrection of the Lord Jesus. And great grace was upon them all." Acts 4:33

"And my speech and my preaching were not with persuasive words of human wisdom, but in demonstration of the Spirit and of power, that your faith should not be in the wisdom of men but in the power of God." 1 Corinthians 2:4-5

Here are more scriptures that reveal what Holy Spirit accomplishes through His power:

- Enables us to boldly proclaim the Gospel.

"On the other hand I am filled with power, with the Spirit of the LORD, and with justice and courage to make known to Jacob his rebellious act, even to Israel his sin." Micah 3:8

"But they were unable to cope with the wisdom and the Spirit with which he was speaking." Acts 6:10

"The statement found approval with the whole congregation; and they chose Stephen, a man full of faith and of the Holy Spirit, and Philip, Prochorus, Nicanor, Timon, Parmenas and Nicolas, a proselyte from Antioch." Acts 6:5

"For God has not given us a spirit of timidity, but of power and love and discipline. Therefore do not be ashamed of the testimony of our Lord or of me His prisoner, but join with me in suffering for the gospel according to the power of God," 2 Timothy 1: 7-8

- Proven effectiveness of the Gospel.

"For our gospel did not come to you in word only, but also in power and in the Holy Spirit and with full conviction; just as you know what kind of men we proved to be among you for your sake." 1 Thessalonians 1:5

"And my message and my preaching were not in persuasive words of wisdom, but in demonstration of the Spirit and of power," 1 Corinthians 2:4

- The power of God.

"But if I cast out demons by the finger of God, then the kingdom of God has come upon you." Luke 11:20

- Qualifies.

"And behold, I am sending forth the promise of My Father upon you; but you are to stay in the city until you are clothed with power from on high." Luke 24:49

- Not in our own power.

"Then he said to me, 'This is the word of the LORD to Zerubbabel saying, 'Not by might nor by power, but by My Spirit,' says the LORD of hosts. 'What are you, O great mountain? Before Zerubbabel you will become a plain; and he will bring forth the top stone with shouts of "Grace, grace to it."'" Zechariah 4: 6-7

- Strengthening through Holy Spirit.

"that He would grant you, according to the riches of His glory, to be strengthened with power through His Spirit in the inner man," Ephesians 3:16

- Resurrected Christ.

"For Christ also died for sins once for all, the just for the unjust, so that He might bring us to God, having been put to death in the flesh, but made alive in the spirit;" 1 Peter 3:18

- Miracles.

"in the power of signs and wonders, in the power of the Spirit; so that from Jerusalem and round about as far as Illyricum I have fully preached the gospel of Christ." Romans 15:19

- Hope.

"Now may the God of hope fill you with all joy and peace in believing, so that you will abound in hope by the power of the Holy Spirit." Romans 15:13

- **Sustains.**

"Restore to me the joy of Your salvation And sustain me with a willing spirit." Psalm 51:12

- **Endowment of Mary.**

"The angel answered and said to her, "The Holy Spirit will come upon you, and the power of the Most High will overshadow you; and for that reason the holy Child shall be called the Son of God." Luke 1:35

- **Beginning of Jesus' ministry.**

"And Jesus returned to Galilee in the power of the Spirit, and news about Him spread through all the surrounding district." Luke 4:14

The power of Holy Spirit, though we see so much scripture revealing His nature, is indescribable. All the ways in which He operates in and through our lives is mind blowing! I am dumbfounded at the thought of people and/or denominations that do not acknowledge His existence. Do they truly know what they are missing in their lives? I am absolutely convinced Holy Spirit is the missing link in the Body of Christ today. His power is almost non-existent, not because He is not available to us, but because we have not allowed Him to freely move in and through us not only in our lives and in our church services, but also to the world. The *anointing* of God is not available, not because He does not desire to be, but because there is "idol worship" within the house of God. God will share His glory with no man, and we cannot just think we can invite Holy Spirit into a place where man is lifted up. Man does not draw God's people, only He can do that.

"And I, if I am lifted up from the earth, will draw all peoples to Myself." John 12:32

The word *anointing* is the supernatural empowerment of God given to the Believer to carry out any given task or assignment,

85

because they are unable to do so in their own power. The *anointing* of the Holy Spirit is given through people to demonstrate God's love and power. God anoints people that love Him more than they love their own lives, and that love others as themselves. As we open our hearts to love others, God's *anointing* flows through us, His power to heal, deliver, set free and save. When we close our hearts to others and grieve Holy Spirit, the flow of His power is stayed from us.

Much of what is done "in the name of Jesus" today is void of the power of God through Holy Spirit. We wonder why so many in the Body of Christ are still riddled with sickness, disease, depression, homosexuality, drug addiction, alcoholism, pornography, adultery and bound by every demon you can possibly think of whose purpose is to keep them in bondage, *even* as born-again Christians. Jesus came that we may be redeemed from sin and given a way to live eternally with the Lord God. Holy Spirit also plays a very important role in the earthly redemptive process for the Believer. He empowers us not only to overcome sin through the Word of God, but also supplies the power to free us from the chains of earthly bondage through the *anointing*.

"It shall come to pass in that day that his burden will be taken away from your shoulder, And his yoke from your neck, And the yoke will be destroyed because of the anointing oil." Isaiah 10:27

"Take My yoke upon you and learn from Me, for I am gentle and lowly in heart, and you will find rest for your souls. For My yoke is easy and My burden is light." Matthew 11: 29-30

As we noted in an earlier chapter, one of the physical characteristics, attributed to Holy Spirit is that of *oil*. Yokes and burdens are destroyed by the *anointing*, or the supernatural power of Holy Spirit. In the physical, we use anointing oil in the Church as a symbol of the natural element, oil, and the supernatural power, Holy Spirit, touching and agreeing with the Word of God for healing, deliverance, ministration and sometimes, salvation. It is an act of faith in God through the outward application of oil, usually placed upon the forehead of a Believer. Now, the power of Holy Spirit is able to destroy every satanic bondage in your life, whether physical, emotional or spiritual, allowing the entranceway of God's love, light and life to transform you forever!

Also Acts 10:38 says, "How God anointed Jesus of Nazareth with the Holy Ghost and with power: who went about doing good." If Jesus needed to be endowed with the power of Holy Spirit, how much more should we His followers? He explained to us that we would do greater works than He did, as He walked upon the earth. How? With the power of Holy Spirit. It is crucial that we understand the power available to us and the purpose for which we have been given the amazing gift of Holy Spirit.

Ezekiel teaches a lesson by his vivid vision of the activity of God portrayed in the wheel within wheels. The moving power within those wheels was the Spirit of God.

"Now as I looked at the living creatures, behold, a wheel was on the earth beside each living creature with its four faces. The appearance of the wheels and their workings was like the color of beryl, and all four had the same likeness. The appearance of their workings was, as it were, a wheel in the middle of a wheel. When they moved, they went toward any one of four directions; they did not turn aside when they went. As for their rims, they were so high they were awesome; and their rims were full of eyes, all around the four of them. When the living creatures went, the wheels went beside them; and when the living creatures were lifted up from the earth, the wheels were lifted up. Wherever the spirit wanted to go, they went, because there the spirit went; and the wheels were lifted together with them, for the spirit of the living creatures was in the wheels. When those went, these went; when those stood, these stood; and when those were lifted up from the earth, the wheels were lifted up together with them, for the spirit of the living creatures was in the wheels." Ezekiel 1:15-21

This is a prophetic picture of how we, too, should be led by Holy Spirit, the Spirit of the Living God within. Ephesians 3:16 says, "That He would grant you, according to the riches of His glory, to be strengthened with power through His Spirit in the inner man." There is unlimited power available to God's people here on earth through the conduit of *Holy Spirit*. Receive His power today!

T.L. Osborn

"The gospel of the kingdom must be preached with evidence; it must be preached as a witness. This can only be done by Christians who are filled with the Holy Spirit."

"Only the power of the Living Christ proclaimed in demonstration of the Holy Spirit, can meet the urgent needs of humanity."
~T.L. Osborn

Chapter 6
The Promise of Holy Spirit

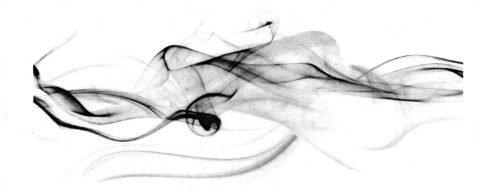

"And being assembled together with them, He commanded them not to depart from Jerusalem, but to wait for the Promise of the Father, "which," He said, "you have heard from Me;" Acts 1:4

Jesus understood His earthly assignment was coming to a conclusion. He taught, inspired, walked and lived as the Word of God before His disciples and all He came in contact with over His earthly ministry. He prepared His followers both physically and spiritually for what they would eventually encounter as He ascended unto Father God. In His resurrected state, before He ascended to Glory, He made this statement to the disciples on the Mount of Olives. The disciples were devastated that He was, indeed, going to be with Father God, as He, as well as the Word of God and the prophets prophesied. What would they do after He was gone? How would they be able to carry on in the midst of great persecution? The very One they were putting their lives upon the line for would no longer be in the earth. What authority and what foundation would they have to witness of the Messiah, the Savior, Jesus the Christ? Though thousands of people saw His miracles and the power and authority in which He spoke, many still refused to believe He was, indeed, the Savior of the world, even after His resurrection. How in the world would these disciples be able to carry on the Gospel of Jesus Christ to the ends of the earth? How you ask? By the *Promise of Holy Spirit!*

"Nevertheless I tell you the truth. It is to your advantage that I go away…" John 16:7

The word *promise* means a declaration that one will do or refrain from doing something specified or a legally binding declaration that gives the person to whom it is made a right to expect or to claim the performance or forbearance of a specified act. The Greek word for promise is *epaggelia*. This word means guaranteed by His own eternal Law (Being). One thing we know of man's promises; they are easily broken with no remorse or means of restoring. When God makes a promise, we can rest assured that not only can we fully trust it, but it is *guaranteed* to come to pass!

"God is not a man, that He should lie, nor a son of man, that He should repent. Has He said, and will He not do? Or has He spoken, and will He not make it good?" Numbers 23:19

"Then said the LORD unto me, Thou hast well seen: for I will hasten my word to perform it." Jeremiah 1:12, KJV

"So shall My word be that goes forth from My mouth; It shall not return to Me void, But it shall accomplish what I please, And it shall prosper in the thing for which I sent it." Isaiah 55:11

"The grass withers, the flower fades, But the word of our God stands forever." Isaiah 40:8

"And being fully convinced that what He had promised He was also able to perform." Romans 4:21

When God speaks something, you can bet your entire life upon it. He does not go around making empty promises just to hear Himself speak. When He speaks it, it *goes forth* and accomplishes *exactly* what He sent it to do. God sent forth Holy Spirit on assignment to encourage, equip and empower the disciples to witness of Jesus Christ to the ends of the earth. He understood they could not do this in their own power or authority; they needed His Spirit within. They would not immediately receive this promise, but they were commanded to tarry, or wait, in Jerusalem until they received Him. It was exactly fifty days from the Crucifixion to Pentecost, but we know from Biblical and historical text that Jesus remained and walked among the disciples for forty days after His Resurrection. So it is safe to say they waited in the *Upper Room* for this "promise" for about ten days.

Prophecy + promise take longer

There are many times that God tells us to wait for His promises over our lives. Though we hear what He desires to do in our lives, and maybe we even received a prophetic word of confirmation, the timeframe from prophecy to promise can, and sometimes will, take much longer than we expected. Jesus did not tell His disciples exactly how long it would take, but they trusted Him and planted their feet firmly in Jerusalem in the *Upper Room* and did what He asked them to do...*wait!* All too often, we get distracted and discouraged, because He is not moving fast enough for us. So, we prematurely move out in the flesh, instead of being led by Holy Spirit. Then, when we find ourselves in a bind, we want to blame God. The problem is not God, but us! If we follow the leading of Holy Spirit, we will be in the right place, at the right time, with the right people, doing and saying the right things. Can you imagine the disciples trying to conjure up Holy Spirit the moment Jesus ascend-

Follow leading of Holy Spirit

ed to Heaven? How foolish they would have felt standing on the Mount of Olives, while *nothing* happened? Looking at one another in disbelief, while one by one, they walk off doubting their Lord and cutting their destiny off by letting it all go? They didn't miss the truth, they missed the timing. *here 5 wks. waiting on*

4-5-18 Thur. Tonies Shandon, CA Been Holy Spirit to move me.

It is imperative that we hear clearly what Holy Spirit is saying to us. If we do not heed His voice, we can miss God's timing for our lives. He gives us clear instruction and direction to go by. He told them to first, remain in Jerusalem. What if they didn't want to stay in Jerusalem? What if Peter and some of the others decided they would rather travel to Bethlehem where Jesus was born to follow "signs" like that of the star that led the wise men to His birth place? What if they felt this was the place where the "promise" would be revealed? How often does God lead us by Holy Spirit to a specific place, but we try everything in our power to get out of going? God knows we have been there several times. Upon our last assignment in Germany, we really felt God wanted us to stay in Germany to help plant churches throughout this country. It was our heart's desire to stay and support our pastor in this region. We thought if God would bless anything; He would surely bless this desire. We were dear friends with the Command Sergeant Major of the military base where we lived and where my husband was stationed. He was also a pastor. He literally made my husband a job working for him and we were ecstatic! God had answered our prayers, or so we thought.

We decided to take leave and travel back home to the states to visit our families, as it had been a while since we had seen them. We spent two weeks in the states and returned to Germany. Upon our arrival, we were informed that we had two weeks to get out of Germany. What? I thought God had orchestrated it so we could stay and fulfill His will in the land of Germany? Not so. In fact, we saw the signs and heard the voice of God, but we rejected it, because our desires were more of a priority than His will. God awakened my husband three nights in a row to a pastor on televi-

our desires more of a priority than His will

saw signs, heard God's voice, we rejected it

sion in the state of Washington. If you know my husband, he is not a "super-spiritual" man. He is a very common sense kind of guy. He loves God and hears His voice, but he usually takes the road of what makes sense. After the second night of God waking him up exactly while this pastor was preaching, it hit him in a strange way. He said, "Deborah, there is something to this." I have to be honest; I wasn't trying to hear anything he was saying. Why? Because God had already made up His mind for us, right? Well, yes, He had, but not in the direction we thought. God was giving my husband a clear and precise direction in which He was leading us, and this was our first sign.

Needless to say, our destination had already been determined for us. This precious pastor, as well as Command Sergeant Major, explained to us that not even the CSM of the military post could stop God's plans for our family. We were on our way on direct military orders to the state of Washington, and sure enough, we joined the very same church my husband saw those three times at exactly 3am in the morning! Now, if that is not the leading of Holy Spirit, I don't know what is? He has a promise set for us all, but we must be in tuned with Holy Spirit to hear clear and precise instruction and direction, so we will be in position to receive all He has for us, as well as to walk completely in His perfect will. From Germany to Washington to Colorado, God had a reason for lining it up the way He ordained. I look back now and I can see His hand literally leading us every step of the way. His promise was unfolding right before our very eyes.

> "And behold, I am sending forth the promise of My Father upon you; but you are to stay in the city until you are clothed with power from on high." Luke 24:49

This is Luke's account of Jesus speaking with His disciples preparing them for His departure. This verse reveals more of the importance of obeying strategic instructions, in order to be in God's divine will for our lives. It also reveals more details, as the

obeying God's strategic instructions, in order to be in God's divine will for our lives verse in Acts only speaks of the "promise"; it does not say the power from on high. This is revealing to them what they will be receiving. Had my husband and I not been given the sign from God leading us to Washington, we could have very well continued to try to fight to stay in Germany or even go elsewhere. We had never been to the state of Washington, nor did we want to go there, but as we slowed down and began to see the pieces of the puzzle coming together, we surrendered to Holy Spirit and chose to trust what God was doing in and through our lives.

We know from the children of Israel that God had a promise for them after bringing them out of Egypt and that was literally to bring them into their Promised Land. Through much impatience and selfishness, they wandered in the wilderness for forty years, delaying the promise for some and completely destroying the promise for many. Rebellion and disobedience keeps us from the promises of God and cuts off the presence of God in our lives. Please don't let that be your testimony. Trust the leading of Holy Spirit and trust that God has a promise for your life that He will bring to pass, as you submit to His voice.

"In Him you also *trusted*, after you heard the word of truth, the gospel of your salvation; in whom also, having believed, you were sealed with the Holy Spirit of promise," Ephesians 1:13, emphasis

The *sealing* of Holy Spirit is a guarantee in the Believer's life that they are, indeed, children of God and at the moment of salvation, this *seal* is made. The Greek word for seal is *shragizo*, meaning to set a seal upon or mark with a seal. A seal can be used to guarantee a document or letter, as well as to indicate ownership or to protect against tampering. God has *sealed* us by the Promise of Holy Spirit; He has marked us with His *seal* of ownership and protection. What love Father God has for His people!

94

"Who also has sealed us and given us the Spirit in our hearts as a guarantee," 1 Corinthians 1:22

The *sealing* of Believers is, in essence, the Promise of Holy Spirit from Father God. Many believe this promise only began before Jesus ascended into Heaven, but God reveals all throughout His Word that He was making promises concerning Holy Spirit in the lives of many Old Testament figures and prophets. Let's take a look at just a few:

1. THE PROMISE OF HOLY SPIRIT IN OLD TESTAMENT PROPHECY.

A. HOLY SPIRIT IN JOEL.

"And it shall come to pass afterward that I will pour out My Spirit on all flesh; Your sons and your daughters shall prophesy, Your old men shall dream dreams, Your young men shall see visions. And also on My menservants and on My maidservants I will pour out My Spirit in those days." Joel 2:28-29

B. HOLY SPIRIT IN ISAIAH.

"For I will pour water on him who is thirsty, And floods on the dry ground; I will pour My Spirit on your descendants, And My blessing on your offspring; They will spring up among the grass like willows by the watercourses.' One will say, 'I am the LORD's'; Another will call himself by the name of Jacob; Another will write with his hand, 'The LORD's,' And name himself by the name of Israel." Isaiah 44:3-5

"Until the Spirit is poured out upon us from on high, and the wilderness becomes a fertile field, And the fertile field is considered as a forest." Isaiah 32:15

"As for Me, this is My covenant with them," says the LORD: "My Spirit which is upon you, and My words which I have put in your mouth shall not depart from your mouth, nor from the mouth of your offspring, nor from the mouth of your off-spring's offspring," says the LORD, "from now and forever." Isaiah 59:21

"The Spirit of the Lord GOD is upon me, Because the LORD has anointed me To bring good news to the afflicted; He has sent me to bind up the brokenhearted, To proclaim liberty to captives And freedom to prisoners; To proclaim the favorable year of the LORD And the day of vengeance of our God; To comfort all who mourn," Isaiah 61:1-2

"The Spirit of the LORD will rest on Him, The spirit of wisdom and understanding, The spirit of counsel and strength, The spirit of knowledge and the fear of the LORD." Isaiah 11:2

C. HOLY SPRIIT IN EZEKIEL.
"I will give you a new heart and put a new spirit within you; I will take the heart of stone out of your flesh and give you a heart of flesh. I will put My Spirit within you and cause you to walk in My statutes, and you will keep My judgments and do them." Ezekiel 36:26-27

"And I will give them one heart, and put a new spirit within them And I will take the heart of stone out of their flesh and give them a heart of flesh," Ezekiel 11:19

"I will put My Spirit within you and you will come to life, and I will place you on your own land. Then you will know that I, the LORD, have spoken and done it," declares the LORD.'" Ezekiel 37:14

"I will not hide My face from them any longer, for I will have poured out My Spirit on the house of Israel," declares the Lord GOD." Ezekiel 39:29

D. HOLY SPIRIT IN ZECHARIAH.

"And I will pour on the house of David and on the inhabitants of Jerusalem the Spirit of grace and supplication; then they will look on Me whom they pierced. Yes, they will mourn for Him as one mourns for his only son, and grieve for Him as one grieves for a firstborn." Zechariah 12:10

E. HOLY SPIRIT IN JEREMIAH.

"Behold, days are coming," declares the Lord, "when I will make a new covenant with the house of Israel and with the house of Judah, not like the covenant which I made with their fathers in the day I took them by the hand to bring them out of the land of Egypt, My covenant which they broke, although I was a husband to them," declares the Lord. "But this is the covenant which I will make with the house of Israel after those days," declares the Lord, "I will put My law within them and on their heart I will write it; and I will be their God, and they shall be My people. "They will not teach again, each man his neighbor and each man his brother, saying, 'Know the Lord,' for they will all know Me, from the least of them to the greatest of them," declares the Lord, "for I will forgive their iniquity, and their sin I will remember no more." Jeremiah 31:31-34

F. HOLY SPIRIT IN DANIEL.

"Then Daniel was brought in before the king. The king spoke, and said to Daniel, "Are you that Daniel who is one of the captives from Judah, whom my father the king brought from Judah? I have heard of you, that the *Spirit of God* is in you, and that light and understanding and excellent wisdom are found in you. Now the wise men, the astrologers, have been brought in before me, that they should read this writing and make known to me its interpretation, but they could not give the interpretation of the thing. And I have heard of you, that you can give interpretations and explain enigmas. Now if you can read the writing and make known to me its interpretation, you

97

shall be clothed with purple and have a chain of gold around your neck, and shall be the third ruler in the kingdom." Daniel 5:13-16, emphasis ~

G. HOLY SPIRIT IN MALACHI.

"But did He not make them one, having a remnant of the Spirit? And why one? He seeks godly offspring. Therefore take heed to your spirit, and let none deal treacherously with the wife of his youth. "For the Lord God of Israel says that He hates divorce, for it covers one's garment with violence," Says the Lord of hosts. "Therefore take heed to your spirit, that you do not deal treacherously." Malachi 2:15-16

2. OTHER REVELATIONS OF THE PROMISE OF HOLY SPIRIT PRE-MESSIAH.

"Gather for Me seventy men from the elders of Israel, whom you know to be the elders of the people and their officers and bring them to the tent of meeting, and let them take their stand there with you. Then I will come down and speak with you there, and I will take of the Spirit who is upon you, and will put Him upon them; and they shall bear the burden of the people with you, so that you will not bear it all alone." Numbers 11:16-17

"Then the Spirit of the LORD will come upon you mightily, and you shall prophesy with them and be changed into another man." 1Samuel 10:6

"And He said, "My presence shall go with you, and I will give you rest." Exodus 33:14

"Then His people remembered the days of old, of Moses Where is He who brought them up out of the sea with the shepherds of His flock? Where is He who put His Holy Spirit in the midst of them, Who caused His glorious arm to go at the right hand of Moses, Who divided the waters before them to make for Himself an everlasting name, Who led them through the depths? Like the horse in the wilderness, they did not stumble;" Isaiah 63:11-14

"As for the promise which I made you when you came out of Egypt, My Spirit is abiding in your midst; do not fear!" Haggai 2:5

So, it is clear that Holy Spirit was a part of every story and every book of the Bible, even if His name was not directly mentioned. We saw that God put the Spirit that was on Moses upon the seventy elders. It is known that the Spirit of God was not with every person in the Old Testament. They either had to be anointed by someone that had Holy Spirit with them, or an impartation was given by God Himself. But nevertheless, the Promise of Holy Spirit was in the Beginning, in Between and surely, in the End. What a privilege to now have unhindered access to Holy Spirit at all times, as we give our lives to Jesus Christ. He loves us so very much and would never leave us alone in this world without His presence within. There is a Promise God has given to us, to live eternally with Him through the shed blood of His precious Son, Jesus Christ. But the Promise Jesus left for us, as He ascended into glory to sit at the right hand of Father God, is available to those that will boldly receive the Gift of *Holy Spirit*. He is the Promise Left for the Believer. Receive Him today into your heart.

Billy Graham

"The Holy Spirit gives liberty to the Christian, direction to the worker, discernment to the teacher, power to the Word, and fruit to faithful service. He reveals the things of Christ."

"The Bible is clear that the Holy Spirit is God Himself."
~Billy Graham

Chapter 7

The Partnership
of Holy Spirit

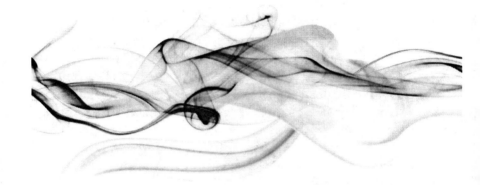

"In all my prayers for all of you, I always pray with joy because of your partnership in the gospel from the first day until now, being confident of this, that *he who began a good work in you* will carry it on to completion until the day of Christ Jesus." Philippians 1:3-9, NIV, emphasis

Though the Godhead: Father, Son and Holy Spirit are One; they serve very unique and distinctive roles in the course of humanity. They are still of the same mind, heart and spirit and work alongside one another to bring you and I, as well as humanity, to an expected end. *"For I know the thoughts that I think toward you, saith the* LORD, *thoughts of peace, and not of evil, to give you an expected end."* (Jeremiah 29:11) Each role is significant and requires the full participation of the other. We see all throughout the Word of God; Father, Son and Holy Spirit working in conjunction with One another to accomplish His will in the earth realm.

Just as in marriage or any other relationship for that matter, it is imperative that we work together to fulfill goals, dreams and ultimately, God's intended purpose for our lives. Many times, someone steps out of the confines of unity and pursues their own selfish agenda, leading to the destruction of the relationship, whether marriage, friendship, business or spiritual connection. In today's world, it is more important to get "connections," instead of forming covenant relationships. The word *connection* means a relationship in which a person, thing, or idea is linked or associated with something else. Connection simply seeks its own. If there is not something mutually beneficial within the relationship, it will usually end. As you see in the definition, it is just an association. The word *association* means a connection or cooperative link between people or organizations. This kind of relationship is very loose; there is not a strong sense of unity or agreement, whereas it becomes a lasting idea.

In contrast, let's look at the word *covenant. Covenant* means agree, especially by lease, deed, or other legal contract; guarantee, pledge or promise. The Biblical definition of covenant stems from the Greek word *berith,* which means treaty, alliance, or league; constitution, ordinance; agreement, pledge or alliance; covenant, as a divine constitution or ordinance with signs or pledges. The word *berith* comes from the word *barah* (in the sense of cutting (like *bara'*); a compact (because made by passing between pieces of flesh)-confederacy, (con-) feder (-ate), covenant, league. This word *covenant* is very important in the life of every Believer. We are not merely connected to God through Holy Spirit, but we are in *covenant* with Him through the shed blood of Jesus Christ, or the cutting away of flesh. Our relationship with Father God is sealed by the Spirit of God. He does not take lightly the sacrifice He made for His people.

How do you see relationship? How do you see marriage? How do you see business partnerships? How do you see spiritual covenant? How you see these things will determine your relationship with God. In fact, you can determine your relationships with others based upon your direct relationship with Father God. I am going somewhere with this, stay with me. The Word of God relates God's love for His people, the Church, as unto earthly marriage; the joining of man and woman as one.

"And He answered and said to them, "Have you not read that He who made them at the beginning 'made them male and female,' and said, 'For this reason a man shall leave his father and mother and be joined to his wife, and the two shall become *one flesh*? So then, they are no longer two but one flesh. Therefore what God has joined together, let not man separate." Matthew 19:4-6, emphasis

When God made covenant with man, Adam, He said it was not good that man be alone, so He made a help meet for him. He "cut the flesh" of Adam, and pulled the rib from his side and made woman. His covenant with Adam was the multiplying and replenishing of the earth through man. In their consummation, Adam and Even became *one flesh*. Through the "shedding of blood" or "cutting away of the flesh," covenant was initiated between man and woman. This is a picture of the covenant God would make in redeeming man from the curse after the Fall through the tearing, or cutting away of the flesh, of our Lord and Savior, Jesus Christ. Blood had to be shed for God's covenant to be enacted. We saw a similar covenant being made between God and Abraham in the sacrificing of his son Isaac on the altar. Abraham was prepared to take a knife and "cut the flesh" of his son in obedience to Father God. This was Abraham's test, and he passed it faithfully.

"Then they came to the place of which God had told him. And Abraham built an altar there and placed the wood in order; and he bound Isaac his son and laid him on the altar, upon the wood. And Abraham stretched out his hand and took the knife to slay his son. But the Angel of the Lord called to him from heaven and said, "Abraham, Abraham!" So he said, "Here I am." And He said, "Do not lay your hand on the lad, or do anything to him; for now I know that you fear God, since you have not withheld your son, your only son, from Me." Genesis 22:9-12

In each of these covenant acts, man partners with God, through obedience to His Word, and establishes an everlasting covenant with Him. The implications of this obedience spans generations upon generations for the glory of God. Partnership between God and man is the most important thing on this earth. All throughout Scripture, we see the testing of man, in order to establish covenant with Father God. Just as in any earthly relationship, trust needs to be established. You don't just trust anyone on the streets with the care of your children, do you? Would you give someone you just met your bank account number or ATM card and trust them to do what you asked of them? The same holds true for God; He tests us in order to determine our faithfulness to Him, as well as our obedience to Him. His ultimate desire is to be on one accord, in agreement with His Creation. This was His ultimate desire in the Garden of Eden, but disobedience led to the separation of God and man.

"I do not pray for these alone, but also for those who will believe in Me through their word; that they all may be one, as You, Father, are in Me, and I in You; that they also may be one in Us, that the world may believe that You sent Me. And the glory which You gave Me I have given them, that they may be one just as We are one: I in them, and You in Me; that they may be made perfect in one, and that the world may know that

You have sent Me, and have loved them as You have loved Me." John 17:20-23

God desires for He and His Creation to be One, even as He and His Son and His Spirit, Holy Spirit, are One. They are in total unison, complete agreement, with one another. All throughout the Gospels, we hear the message of Jesus Christ concerning unity and agreement with His Father in Heaven. Everything He did, He did as he heard Father God speak through the vessel, or conduit, of Holy Spirit. Let's look at a few scriptures that reveal Father, Son and Holy Spirit working in partnership in the earth.

"I, therefore, the prisoner of the Lord, beseech you to walk worthy of the calling with which you were called, with all lowliness and gentleness, with longsuffering, bearing with one another in love, endeavoring to keep the unity of the Spirit in the bond of peace. There is one body and one Spirit, just as you were called in one hope of your calling; one Lord, one faith, one baptism; one God and Father of all, who is above all, and through all, and in you all." Ephesians 4:1-6

God would never expect us to do anything He has not already done. His blueprint of marriage and relationship in the earth is based upon His agreement with His Son and His Spirit, Holy Spirit. Jesus says He only speaks what the Father tells Him to speak:

"For I have not spoken on My own authority; but the Father who sent Me gave Me a command, what I should say and what I should speak. And I know that His command is everlasting life. Therefore, whatever I speak, just as the Father has told Me, so I speak." John 12:49-50

"Then Jesus answered and said to them, "Most assuredly, I say to you, the Son can do nothing of Himself, but what He sees the Father do; for whatever He does, the Son also does in like manner. For the Father loves the Son, and shows Him all things that He Himself does; and He will show Him greater works than these, that you may marvel." John 5:19-20

"Then Jesus said to them, "When you lift up the Son of Man, then you will know that I am He, and that I do nothing of Myself; but as My Father taught Me, I speak these things." John 8:28

Some refute the existence of Holy Spirit in these scriptures, but what we fail to acknowledge, or realize, is that when the "dove" descended upon Jesus at His baptism, this was representative of Holy Spirit coming to dwell within our Lord and Savior in the earth realm. Jesus was God as man, but He still needed the supernatural empowerment of Holy Spirit in order to operate fully in His assignment here on earth. When He says He spoke only what He heard His Father speak, how do you think He heard this? Yes, through Holy Spirit. Holy Spirit was leading, instructing and directing Jesus every step of the way. He is covenanted with Father and Spirit to fulfill God's purposes for humanity. They are not separate, but have the same heart, mind and purpose, and work together in unity to bring God's will upon the earth, just as it is in Heaven. (Matthew 6:10)

So, too, is His desire for man. He wants us walking in complete unity with Him, through His Word, Jesus and His Spirit, Holy Spirit. We should be saying only what we hear the Spirit of God saying to us not only through the Word, *logos*, but also through His Spirit, *rhema*. The triumvirate purpose and partnership is absolute genius, orchestrated by the Creator Himself. We see His *watermark* all throughout scripture and we see it in our everyday lives, in every area of life. This blueprint of unity is God's designed purpose for our lives. The Word of God says in Psalm 133:1-3:

"Behold, how good and how pleasant it is for brethren to dwell together in unity! It is like the precious oil upon the head, running down on the beard, the beard of Aaron, running down on the edge of his garments. It is like the dew of Hermon, Descending upon the mountains of Zion; For there the LORD commanded the blessing—Life forevermore."

Again, the oil here represents Holy Spirit and His partnership with Father God and Jesus in the unity of mankind. What a team! I pray often for unity not only in marriage, but also in the Body of Christ. We have to understand that as the original Creation revealed God's will for unity amongst man and woman in the foundation of marriage, this is where each and every one of us must begin. It is God's will that each of us not only covenant with Him, but also with one another. He said that it is not good for man to be alone. God's design is marriage. It is the closest thing on earth to the covenant we have in God.

So many today feel it unnecessary to get married for one reason or another. Marriage is under attack more than anything today, even in the Church. Divorce rates have skyrocketed within the Body of Christ. Some would even contend that the divorce rate in the Church has exceeded that of the world. Forty or fifty years ago, marriage was still a very important covenant between man and woman, until the Feminist Movement, or Women's Liberation Movement, came to fruition. In the 1960's-1970's, women rallied for equal rights between them and their male counterparts. They fought for reproductive rights, domestic violence, maternity leave, equal pay, women's suffrage, sexual harassment, and sexual violence. It originally focused on dismantling workplace inequality, but what it succeeded in doing was singlehandedly dismantling the sanctity of marriage all over the world. It not only distorted the view of man in woman's eyes, but it also blinded women to what they were doing to themselves. This was a scheme orchestrated by the enemy of our souls, our adversary, Satan. He understood completely the unity God desired for mankind in the Garden. He knew the consequences of a divided family and what it would do to the image of God in the earth realm. I have to say, we have spiraled completely in the wrong direction of God's original intent.

Men have become the enemy, instead of Satan. With women changing laws and the landscape of our society, men have been emasculated in every sense of the word. A man's job is to take care of his family and protect them in every way. When a woman feels she is equal to man, she no longer needs him to care for her financially, let alone protect her. She is empowered to believe she can do all of this on her own now. When the man is left without purpose, he is tempted to find love and respect in other women. Some men turn to alcohol and drugs to ease the pain of their hopelessness. In many cases, this causes a downward spiral that leads many men to prison. Now, women are really left to be the financial provider of their homes, caretaker of their children and spiritual advisor in the home. The entire burden that used to rest upon the man is now on the shoulders of women. Frustration, bitterness, resentment, anger and hate fester to the point where these women become fed up and either stray from their marriages, or ultimately, divorce their husbands. So many men in prison become statistics of a failed marriage or relationship and the enemy sets on his course to steal, kill and destroy any self-worth left inside of a man.

Rape is inevitable for most men in the prison system. Once a man's masculinity is stolen, it is seen as the end for many. Homosexuality is a tool of the enemy to completely destroy God's image in the earth realm. His desire is to distort the beauty of Creation and to impale the image of the Creator. After all of this, we are able to clearly see the plot of the enemy to wreak havoc upon God's Creation. Marriages are destroyed, men and women are deceived into changing their identity, and children are not being born, either through homosexuality or even abortion. The enemy wants to remove every trace of God's image in the earth realm. As I stated in the beginning, there is a dark spirit at work in the earth and its purpose is to kill, steal and destroy. I will fully deal with this spirit at the conclusion of this book.

It is only through the partnership of Holy Spirit that we are able to discern what is taking place in the world today. When our eyes have been opened through Holy Spirit, much will change in this dark, deceitful age. Holy Spirit works in conjunction with God to break through the chains of darkness, destroy yokes and to bring His people out of bondage. I firmly believe that Holy Spirit is the missing key that will unlock the many promises of God in the earth, as well as to restore all that the enemy has stolen from God's people. Marriages will be restored, broken lives will be healed, fathers will return to the helm of their children's lives, blind eyes will be opened to the way in which they were born and our society will turn back to the Lord and morals will be reinstated. I see it happening even as I write this book. Holy Spirit is moving and speaking to God's people. Renewal, refreshing, restoration, resurrection, redemption and reconciliation are all taking place through the partnership of Holy Spirit with the God of Creation. I don't know about you, but I am excited to be living in these times. It may look dark, but I am assured that our light can shine the brightest in such times.

Even as Holy Spirit is restoring the lives and fabric of our society, He, too, is working on the Body of Christ. I don't know about you, but I am really getting tired of the old, stale duplications and "batting at the air" sermons and prophecies I see and hear in so many forums across the world. People are building sermons and prophecies off of television series titles, off of other people's messages, and off of current world events, instead of hearing the pure, authentic voice of Holy Spirit and speaking as He speaks. The Church of the Living God in the earth realm is like the "Valley of Dry Bones" coined in Ezekiel. The only way these bones will "live" and come to the full fruition of God's intent in the earth is through the authentic leading and breathing of Holy Spirit.

"The hand of the Lord came upon me and brought me out in the Spirit of the Lord, and set me down in the midst of the valley; and it was full of bones. Then He caused me to pass by them all around, and behold, there were very many in the open valley; and indeed they were very dry. And He said to me, "Son of man, can these bones live?" So I answered, "O Lord God, You know."

"Again He said to me, "Prophesy to these bones, and say to them, 'O dry bones, hear the word of the Lord! Thus says the Lord God to these bones: "Surely I will cause breath to enter into you, and you shall live. I will put sinews on you and bring flesh upon you, cover you with skin and put breath in you; and you shall live. Then you shall know that I am the Lord.""

"So I prophesied as I was commanded; and as I prophesied, there was a noise, and suddenly a rattling; and the bones came together, bone to bone. Indeed, as I looked, the sinews and the flesh came upon them, and the skin covered them over; but there was no breath in them. Also He said to me, "Prophesy to the breath, prophesy, son of man, and say to the breath, 'Thus says the Lord God: "Come from the four winds, O breath, and breathe on these slain, that they may live.""

"So I prophesied as He commanded me, and breath came into them, and they lived, and stood upon their feet, an exceedingly great army. Then He said to me, "Son of man, these bones are the whole house of Israel. They indeed say, 'Our bones are dry, our hope is lost, and we ourselves are cut off!' Therefore prophesy and say to them, 'Thus says the Lord God: "Behold, O My people, I will open your graves and cause you to come up from your graves, and bring you into the land of Israel. Then you shall know that I am the Lord, when I have opened your graves, O My people, and brought you up from your graves. I will put My Spirit in you, and you shall live, and I will place you in your own land. Then you shall know that I, the Lord, have spoken it and performed it," says the Lord.'"
Ezekiel 37:1-13

This is truly a prophetic picture of the Church today. It was a prophecy of God restoring the house of Israel to her glory, but it is also a prophetic look at the restoration and reconciliation of His glory within the Body of Christ, as well. We are in some of the shakiest times the Church has seen. We are literally watching Scripture unfold before our very eyes; prophecy being manifested in our midst. The great falling away has begun and to see so many spiritual leaders falling, and many more of their followers joining their ranks, is devastating.

"Now the Spirit expressly says that in latter times some will depart from the faith, giving heed to deceiving spirits and doctrines of demons, speaking lies in hypocrisy, having their own conscience seared with a hot iron, forbidding to marry, and commanding to abstain from foods which God created to be received with thanksgiving by those who believe and know the truth." 1 Timothy 1:1-3

The Spirit of God, Holy Spirit, warns us of this great falling away, or Apostasy, that will come to the Body of Christ. I only saw this scripture at surface level, until I began to see some of my very own spiritual leaders and mentors falling away from the faith they taught and imparted within me. Several of them have prophesied into and over my life, my family, my business and the call of God on my life. I don't doubt one bit that they were hearing from Holy Spirit concerning my life, because much has already come to pass. It is just devastating to see such gifted and faithful leaders now deceived and turning away from Jesus Christ. I truly want to encourage, exhort and equip Believers in these last days to stay close to Holy Spirit. He is speaking to us and giving us discernment to know what is God and what is not God. Just as this scripture in 1 Timothy reveals to us, these are some very dark days. If we go on a little further in this chapter, it tells us:

"If you instruct the brethren in these things, you will be a good minister of Jesus Christ, nourished in the words of faith and of the good doctrine which you have carefully followed."
1 Timothy 4:6

Don't ever feel that you are being disloyal, or that you are betraying someone that has taught and poured into your spiritual life. If they have fallen away from the faith and the Word of God you know to be Truth, then it is your duty to warn others of such false teachings. And Holy Spirit will be right there beside you, partnering with you, to lead others to the Truth. I have to say I have had a very eventful last decade walking with Holy Spirit and partnering with Him in the assignment God has placed upon my life. I have literally had to learn to follow Holy Spirit at all costs; being led, directed and challenged by Him to stand up and out against apostasy and false teachings within the Church. Though it has been a difficult journey, He has taught me so much and partnered with me in this assignment. We look at the dynamic of Holy Spirit in partnership with God, but there is also another realm of Holy Spirit partnering with God's people to help them fulfill their God-given assignments and ultimate destiny. He is with us everywhere we go; He will never leave us nor forsake us. He is fully engaged in every area of our lives if we allow Him the opportunity.

"Where can I go from Your Spirit? Or where can I flee from Your presence? If I ascend into heaven, You are there; If I make my bed in hell, behold, You are there. If I take the wings of the morning, And dwell in the uttermost parts of the sea, Even there Your hand shall lead me, And Your right hand shall hold me." Psalm 139:7-10

My God! What a tremendous gift that God would give us His Spirit, Holy Spirit, to walk with us, in partnership, throughout our lifetime. No matter where we are; no matter what we are going through; no matter the glorious ups or devastating downs, He is completely with us and for us. He is not here to take away from our lives, but absolutely here to enhance and embolden us to complete our race here on earth. As a born-again Believer, how can you not accept such a gift from Father God?

"If you then, being evil, know how to give good gifts to your children, how much more will your Father who is in heaven give good things to those who ask Him!" Matthew 7:11

God wants the best for His children. He gave us His only Son, and He left His precious Holy Spirit with us to keep on running this earthly race. What a loving Father! I urge you to accept and acknowledge Holy Spirit as your partner in this spiritual walk. Every step of your life; every decision you will ever have to make, can be led by our Partner in this walk of faith...*Holy Spirit.*

Dr. Martin Luther King, Jr.

"We need to pledge ourselves anew to the cause of Christ. We must capture the spirit of the early church. Wherever the early Christians went, they made a triumphant witness for Christ. Whether on the village streets or in the city jails, they daringly proclaimed the good news of the gospel."

"Use me, God. Show me how to take who I am, who I want to be, and what I can do, and use it for a purpose greater than myself."
~Martin Luther King Jr.

Chapter 8
Relationship & Intimacy with the Father

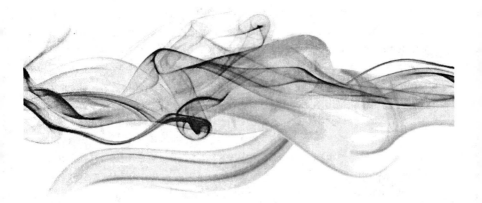

"and the Holy Spirit descended upon Him in bodily form like a dove, and a voice came out of heaven, "You are My beloved Son, in You I am well-pleased." Luke 3:22

To know the love of God is absolutely the greatest gift anyone will ever experience. He spoke the universe into existence out of love. He fashioned the heavens, the seas, the mountains, every animal of every kind, a plethora of ocean life, the millions of species of plants and ultimately, mankind with great care, precision and yes, love. We were created to Worship Him. We were formed to bring glory to His name. We were shaped for relationship and intimacy with the Creator of the Universe, our Father God. As we spoke in the last chapter, God desires covenant with His people, not a mere connection. Covenant brings intimacy into relationship. The word *intimacy* means close familiarity or friendship; closeness. It is also linked to sexual togetherness, intimate love. The Greek word for intimacy is *koinónia*, which means fellowship, partnership, contributory help, and participation, sharing in, communion, spiritual fellowship or a fellowship in the spirit.

Just as we spoke in the last chapter, God desires that we are in partnership with Him through Holy Spirit, as well as a reciprocal fellowship between God and man in fulfilling His plan in the earth realm. This cannot be obtained without a personal and intimate relationship with the Father. We cannot view Father, Son and Holy Spirit as tools we use to get Heaven, or to get our way here in the world. Sadly, this is the "relationship" many Believers have with God. In reality, this is no relationship at all. It is a one-sided antagonism designed to promote self-sufficiency within man in this world. It provides man with as much leeway as possible here in the earth with little or no input from the heavenly realm. This is pretty much saying, "I want to go to heaven, but I don't want to surrender my will to God. I want to have as much control in my life as possible without interference."

So many miss out on the fullness of God's blessing when they refuse to be in relationship with Him. Others only see salvation as "fire insurance;" they may not necessarily have faith in God, but have fear in the back of their minds that says, "What will happen if I am wrong?" Either way, they are missing out on the greatest relationship they will ever experience in their lives, and *intimacy* is a crucial part of that process.

Let's look at four types of intimacy. According to the University of Florida Counseling and Wellness Center[vii], intimacy is a process – not a thing. It takes place over time and is not stagnant.

In fact, any kind of stagnation in a relationship kills intimacy. Intimacy can also take many forms.

- ❖ **Cognitive/Intellectual**-where two people exchange thoughts, share ideas and enjoy similarities and differences between their opinions
- ❖ **Experiential**- where people get together to actively involve themselves with each other, probably saying very little to each other, not sharing any thoughts or many feelings, but being involved in mutual activities with one another
- ❖ **Emotional**- where two persons can comfortably share their feelings with each other or when they empathize with the feelings of the other person, really try to understand and try to be aware of the other person's emotional side
- ❖ **Sexual**- includes a broad range of sensuous activity and is much more than just sexual intercourse. It's any form of sensual expression with each other

Understanding what natural intimacy is will help us to better understand how God sees spiritual intimacy with His people. We see a progression, or process, through each of these forms of intimacy. You will have many relationships in life, and not all will have the same level of closeness and sharing. Some will grow over time and lead to deeper friendships and/or relationships. As in any relationship, you get out of it what you put in it. You cannot expect to receive if you never give. As Believers in Jesus Christ, we cannot expect to receive the promises of God if we are not in relationship with Him. Obedience to God's Word and intimacy with Father God through Holy Spirit brings great benefits. This is not necessarily material benefits, but more importantly, spiritual, allowing us the peace, joy, comfort, faith, love and yes, intimacy with God that is eternal.

"We proclaim to you what we have seen and heard, so that you also may have fellowship with us. And our fellowship is with the Father and with His Son, Jesus Christ." 1 John 1:3

Fellowship, or intimacy, is very important to Father God. He longs to speak with His people; He longs to be in constant communion with His Creation. Can you imagine being married and never speaking with your spouse? Can you fathom never sleeping in the same bed or making love to one another? What kind of marriage is this? It is no marriage at all. All throughout the Word of God, we see the word "know" in relation to intimacy with God, as well as between husband and wife. This is the Hebrew word *yada*, meaning to enter into covenant with one another. This word holds strong meaning. In Ancient days, if a king broke covenant with another dignitary, it meant severe consequences, even death. Abraham showed great covenant with God in the fact that he was willing to sacrifice, kill, his son Isaac. He had great intimacy with God and chose obedience over sacrifice. Our Lord and Savior, Jesus Christ was obedient, even to the point of death on the Cross. (Philippians 2:8)

Many people have issues with commitment, whether in marriage, friendship, business or spiritual spheres. Commitment is a huge part of covenant and subsequently, intimacy. If I hold back enough, I won't have to be bound by any relational ties. I can do and go as I please and I won't have to answer to anyone, or be held accountable. Accountability is an important part of covenant relationship. *Accountability* is the fact or condition of being accountable; responsibility; liability or answerability. This is a tough word for many people. They don't mind being in relationship, but refuse to answer to anyone other than themselves. This is a very dangerous place to be for a Believer. The enemy is very deceitful and will use this against us and keep us from the relationships God has ordained for our lives to guard us from sin and disobedience. *Accountability* is a great gift and benefit for anyone. If we truly love someone, we will be there to hold them accountable, so they are able to get back into the will of God for their lives. Holy Spirit serves as a very important aspect of intimacy, covenant, fellowship, communion and yes, even accountability. He is able to lead us by His voice and soften our hearts to receive from others, as well as God. Holy Spirit is able to break down communicational barriers that usually hinder us from close friendships, intimate relationships, as well as spiritual covenant with man and God.

One aspect that will keep us from experiencing intimacy and relationship with God is the lack of vulnerability. The word *vulnerability* means capable of or susceptible to being wounded or hurt, as by a weapon; open to temptation, persuasion, or censure. Most people refuse to enter into covenant with someone, because they are afraid of being hurt. We must be willing to let our guards down if we are, indeed, to find fulfillment in our natural, as well as spiritual relationships. As we submit our lives to Father God, Holy Spirit guards our hearts and gives us confidence and assurance of God's love for us, as well as provides us with faith and trust to "do it scared" at times. Faith does not mean that we will always fully trust what God is saying to us. If we did, then it wouldn't be faith. Faith is defined in Hebrews 11:1 as:

"Now faith is the substance of things hoped for, the evidence of things not seen." Hebrews 11:1

To trust God in this manner requires great *intimacy*. We may not understand what He is doing, but because we know He loves us and has nothing but good thoughts toward us, we choose to trust and have faith in Him. As we learn to continue to trust Him, we will begin to see a pattern of His faithfulness in and over our lives. What a joy it is to be in relationship with the God of Creation!

Intimacy and relationship with God provides access to areas others are not privy to or privileged to walk in. As I stated earlier, there are multiple benefits to being in relationship with Him. Holy Spirit provides us spiritual access into places and situations that we normally would not be able to go in our natural ability or influence. This is not necessarily for our own benefit, but to accomplish, or fulfill, God's perfect plan for our lives, as well as for humanity.

"For through Him we both have access by one Spirit to the Father." Ephesians 2:18

To have *access* means permission, liberty, or ability to enter, approach, or pass to and from a place or to approach or communicate with a person or thing; freedom or ability to obtain or make use of something; a way or means of access. This definition made my spirit leap and this is not even the Biblical meaning! Intimacy and relationship with God through Holy Spirit affords us a means to pass to and from, as well as in and through the earthly and heavenly realms. Let's look at the Biblical definition of access. The word "access" in the Greek is *prosagógé* meaning approach, access or admission; intimate (face to face) interaction or having an 'audience' (direct access) with God. Okay, now if this does not stir your spirit up, I don't know what will?

Many of the elite in society, as well as many celebrities and wealthy people pride themselves on their VIP statuses and *all access* passes to the hottest spots around the world. It is always the "Who's Who" of society and if you don't have the proper credentials to get in, you will most likely be turned away at the door. But there are "doors" that even they cannot enter into without the access only Holy Spirit can provide! Glory to God! I would not trade the access God has given me into the spiritual realm for any amount of money, fame, or notoriety this world has to offer!

"Therefore, having been justified by faith, we have peace with God through our Lord Jesus Christ, through whom also we have access by faith into this grace in which we stand, and rejoice in hope of the glory of God." Romans 5:1-2

Nothing can compare to the intimacy Father God gives to His children; those in covenant relationship with Him. The rich and famous think they have it all, yet they are lacking peace, hope, joy and authentic love. Many famous people near the end of their lives will tell you that if they had to do it over again, they would choose peace, instead of prosperity; love, instead of lust; humility, instead of haughtiness. It is truly magnificent when someone runs into the life changing, transformative power of God through Holy Spirit! For these people, they have nothing left to achieve. They have made their fortunes, traveled all over the world, own mansions, luxury cars, expensive jewelry, clothes and feel as if there is nothing left to buy or obtain. There is a gaping void within their lives and money cannot fill it. In many of these cases, you will see these multi-millionaires, or billionaires, begin to give away their fortunes to help the poor, the widows and the orphans, as well as giving to many charitable organizations and philanthropic work around the globe. In their serving others, they are introduced to an intimate God that absolutely adores them and wants to shower them with His love and light. I have met a few of these people, and it is such a testament of the leading and guiding of Holy Spirit and His beautiful work in and through our lives.

> "to the intent that now the manifold wisdom of God might be made known by the church to the principalities and powers in the heavenly places, according to the eternal purpose which He accomplished in Christ Jesus our Lord, in whom we have boldness and access with confidence through faith in Him."
> Ephesians 3:10-12

There is a place of boldness and confidence that you will operate in, as you grow closer in relationship with Father God. Through intimacy, you will encounter an authentic relationship with the Lord. The word *authentic* means worthy of acceptance or belief as conforming to or based on fact; made or done the same way as an original; not false or imitation; true to one's own personality, spirit, or character. In a world full of so much manipulation and deceit, it is paramount to know what is authentic and what is counterfeit. An authentic relationship with God stems from a bold and confident declaration of surrender to Jesus Christ, the Son of the Living God. It is in this affirmation that authenticity is established. How can we know this? The Word of God says even the demons tremble and believe:

> "You believe that there is one God. You do well. Even the demons believe—and tremble!" James 2:19

Ray C. Stedman in his book "Authentic Christianity" shares much about the idea of authenticity and how it will completely transform the life of a follower of Christ. He attests that to truly be authentic, we must move beyond religion, doctrine, rules, and rituals, and move into the life changing experience of being intimately connected to God through Jesus Christ at the very core of our being. He states:

> "Many influences and experiences may lead us to an encounter with Jesus Christ. Those influences and experiences may even be intensely religious and theologically profound-but until a person responds to the promise of Christ and receives Him as Lord, there can be no spiritual reality, no eternal life."[viii]

Be alert, watch, pray and discern. It is not that hard to recognize a counterfeit. There are several ways in which God will give you discernment, through Holy Spirit, to stay on the path of true, intimate and authentic fellowship with Him. Probably one of the most important ways is through Prayer. God is a God of communication. He loves to speak with His children. Just as in marriage, if you spend years of your life with someone, you should be able to discern if your husband or your wife would say or do something someone is accusing them of saying or doing. Someone can approach you and say, "Your husband was caught hitting a woman at work." Knowing your husband and having history with him, you know he has never once put his hands upon you, let alone anyone else. So, immediately, you are not going to believe this person, but you are going to get to the source to find out what is really going on. The same holds true with God. If you are in prayer, intimate fellowship and covenant, with the Father, you will know Him and His character. You will know when someone or something is out of order, because it does not "look" like your Father.

The second way God allows us to discern is through His Word. What is written, as we saw earlier, was inspired by Holy Spirit through holy men of God. We understand that the fullness of God is surely not contained with the Word of God, but it is absolutely enough of Him that we are able to know Him intimately. Anytime someone professes to be a Christian and takes away or adds to the Scripture, we should have a red flag up ready to defend the Truth. I am not saying we need to confront every person that strays away from the Word of God, but what we are required to do is mark that individual and guard ourselves against deceit. So many pastors and spiritual leaders today are falling away from their first love. The holy scriptures are no longer their final authority, and many are now preaching and teaching their own doctrines and beliefs. It is imperative that we know the Word of God for ourselves, so as not to become deceived. In knowing the scriptures, this will also allow us the knowledge of His character.

If a pastor or spiritual leader preaches another doctrine other than what we have known and have been taught, if we know the Word of God, we can easily detect the counterfeit, but what about the spirit of preaching and teaching? If we know God's attributes through the Word, then we will also know that a spirit of condemnation, or attack, from anyone calling himself a believer, let alone a pastor, is not of God. If it does not "sound" like Him, then you will know, or discern, a counterfeit spirit. The Spirit must line up with the Word. If it does not, it is not authentic. The spirit of authenticity in a Believer requires an intertwining of Grace and Truth. Meaning, you cannot have one without the other and call it

God. I have witnessed far too much spiritual abuse across the pulpits in America, as well as around the world.

Prayer and continual meditation and study upon the Word of God are the foundation of intimacy and relationship with Father God. As we remain grounded in them, we are able to guard ourselves against such spiritual abuse and not be moved out of our position in Christ. As we stay in constant communication with God, through Holy Spirit, I believe we will continue in authentic intimacy with Him.

Another aspect of intimacy is that of friendship. *Friendship* is defined as the state of being friends; the quality or state of being friendly. The Greek word *philos* is defined biblically as a friend; someone dearly loved (prized) in a personal, intimate way; a trusted confidant, held dear in a close bond of personal affection. There are two Greek words that combine to define the term 'friend of God' in the Word, *theos* and *philos* (Theophilos). Theophilus was a friend of Luke's; the Gospel of Luke and Acts were dedicated to this man.

"It seemed good to me also, having had perfect understanding of all things from the very first, to write to you an orderly account, most excellent Theophilus," Luke 1:3

"The former account I made, O Theophilus, of all that Jesus began both to do and teach," Acts 1:1

This man had to have been a very close friend and partner in the Gospel with Luke for him to acknowledge him in both of these books. He must have evidently won the trust and admiration of Luke. But there is only one person in the Word of God that is given the privilege of being called the "friend of God" and that is Abraham. Let's look at Isaiah 41:8:

"But you, Israel, are My servant, Jacob whom I have chosen, the descendants of Abraham My friend."

What an honor to be called God's friend! Abraham, from the day God called him out of his country, the Ur of the Chaldees, obeyed the voice of the Lord and followed Him by blind faith. There was something keenly distinct that signaled obedience in this man from the land of Babylonia. He had a witness in his spirit that this was the God of Heaven summoning him for his assignment. Obedience is a crucial part of intimacy with God. You cannot be in intimate fellowship with God while in disobedience. Disobedience in the life of a Believer is counted as sin, and we know that sin separates us from Father God.

"And the Scripture was fulfilled which says, "Abraham believed God, and it was accounted to him for righteousness."And he was called the friend of God." James 2:23, emphasis

Obedience is defined as compliance with an order, request, or law or submission to another's authority. The Hebrew word for "obedience" is *shama*, which simply means to hear. The Greek is *hupakoé*, meaning obedience, submissiveness, compliance. Abraham simply heard a Word from God and went. In fact, Scripture reveals that Abraham did not even question the Lord, but heard, complied, submitted and obeyed. Abraham was from an idolatrous city, full of sin and idol worship. His father, Terah, was an idol maker; he constructed many forms of idols and sold them to the pagan worshipers of this city.

"By faith Abraham obeyed when he was called to go out to the place which he would receive as an inheritance. And he went out, not knowing where he was going." Hebrews 11:8

Let's look at several scriptures that reveal some very important aspects of friendship:

The friendship between David and Jonathan is probably the most noted in the Word of God. Their souls were knit together; they were in covenant and their lives were connected for a greater purpose than their own.

"The soul of Jonathan was knit to the soul of David, and Jonathan loved him as his own soul." 1 Samuel 18:1

A true friend is hard to find. Many seek approval and acceptance in many circles, instead of genuine friendship. If you find one or two good friends in life, you are truly blessed.

"A man of many companions may come to ruin, but there is a friend who sticks closer than a brother." Proverbs 18:24

There is no wisdom in surrounding yourself with people that will tell you what you want to hear, instead of what you need to hear. These are "yes" people; they feed our pride and our egos and do not have our best interests at heart. We need friends, true friends that will push us toward our destiny in Christ Jesus. They will speak the "hard things," in order for us to stay on the narrow path.

"Faithful are the wounds of a friend; profuse are the kisses of an enemy." Proverbs 27:6

Fellowship is an important key to intimacy and relationship. Isolation is a trick of the enemy to shut us off from the blessing of God. God uses people in the earth as 'vessels' to walk with us through times of victory, as well as times of turmoil. There is great comfort in godly friendship.

"Two are better than one, because they have a good reward for their toil. For if they fall, one will lift up his fellow. But woe to him who is alone when he falls and has not another to lift him up!" Ecclesiastes 4:9-10

What are you willing to sacrifice for someone else? Friendship is not simply association, it is relationship. It is not what we seek to get out of the relationship, but what we are willing to put in. Many will call you their brother or sister, or friend, but when times get tough, they are the first ones to run. Cherish those that remain with you when all others disappear. They will stand with you in your assignment for God, and will go to great lengths to fight with you through your battles.

"Greater love has no one than this, that someone lay down his life for his friends." John 15:13

Surround yourself with people that have the same level of faith, if not greater than you. People with the same heart, mind, faith and spirit will stand in agreement with the call of God upon your life, and vice versa. They will love you, and correct you. Their correction is not to cut, but to sharpen what is inside of you. These kinds of friends are priceless!

"Iron sharpens iron; so one man sharpens another." Proverbs 27:17

We all have our pitfalls in life. We have our ups and we have our downs. To have a friend that will love us through our good and bad is truly a gift from God.

"A friend loves at all times, and a brother is born for adversity." Proverbs 17:17

We can also see reference in the Gospels to Jesus seeing His disciples as His friends.

"No longer do I call you servants, for a servant does not know what his master is doing; but I have called you friends, for all things that I heard from My Father I have made known to you." John 15:15

Most people automatically perceive the word servant as something negative. Nobody wants to be someone's servant, right? The word *servant* is defined as one that serves others (a public servant); especially one that performs duties about the person or home of a master or personal employer. The Greek word for "servant" is *diakonos*, meaning a servant or minister. This is where we get the office of deacon in the Church. The Hebrew is *ebed*, meaning bondage, bondman, bondservant, and manservant; slave.

When we surrender our lives to God, we are no longer considered our own. Our lives are now lived in complete service to our Lord and Savior. Being a deacon or a minister, or having titles in the Church is coveted by many. They view these titles as glorious, as it gives them prominence. This is truly a distorted picture of what God really calls us to when He releases us into true servant leadership. We are called to "die" to self, as we take on the body of Christ. We are called as servants, or slaves to Christ, not in a demeaning or subservient manner, but in service to the One that was beaten and bruised for our iniquities; the One that gave His own life for our sins. True intimacy and relationship with God comes as we become servants to His will.

Let's see how God views a true servant:

"For even the Son of Man did not come to be served, but to serve, and to give His life a ransom for many." Mark 10:45

"Have this attitude in yourselves which was also in Christ Jesus, who, although He existed in the form of God, did not regard equality with God a thing to be grasped, but emptied Himself, taking the form of a bond-servant, and being made in the likeness of men." Philippians 2:5-8

"Let no one seek his own good, but that of his neighbor." 1 Corinthians 10:24

"And there arose also a dispute among them as to which one of them was regarded to be greatest. And He said to them, "The kings of the Gentiles lord it over them; and those who have authority over them are called 'Benefactors.' "But it is not this way with you, but the one who is the greatest among you must become like the youngest, and the leader like the servant." Luke 22:24-30

"Were you called while a slave? Do not worry about it; but if you are able also to become free, rather do that. For he who was called in the Lord while a slave, is the Lord's freedman; likewise he who was called while free, is Christ's slave. You were bought with a price; do not become slaves of men."
1 Corinthians 7:21-31

"Let a man regard us in this manner, as servants of Christ and stewards of the mysteries of God." 1 Corinthians 4:1

"So when He had washed their feet, and taken His garments and reclined at the table again, He said to them, "Do you know what I have done to you? "You call Me Teacher and Lord; and you are right, for so I am. "If I then, the Lord and the Teacher, washed your feet, you also ought to wash one another's feet."
John 13:12-15

What a view of intimacy and relationship with the Father! Did you know each of these things would draw you closer to Him? Why did we break off from teaching on Holy Spirit to understand intimacy and relationship with Father God? Because one, you cannot separate them; they are all One. Learning how to be vulnerable to the leading of Holy Spirit will grant you access into realms you would never imagine! And secondly, to know Him is to know His Spirit, Holy Spirit. I believe that as we grow closer to the Father, we will not only gain a clear perspective in our assignments, but we will also develop a greater level of intimacy in all of our earthly relationships.

What a joy it is to be in *koinónia* (intimacy, fellowship, covenant & relationship) with the Father through *Holy Spirit!*

"Though one may be overpowered by another, two can withstand him. And a threefold cord is not quickly broken." Ecclesiastes 4:12

Leonard Ravenhill

"Yearly we use mountains of paper and rivers of ink reprinting dead men's brains; while the living Holy Ghost is seeking for men to trample underfoot their own learning, deflate their inflated ego."

"A man who is intimate with God is not intimidated by man."
~Leonard Ravenhill

Chapter 9
Holy Spirit: Helper/Teacher

"But I tell you the truth, it is to your advantage that I go away; for if I do not go away, the Helper will not come to you; but if I go, I will send Him to you." John 16:17

One of the greatest names used in conjunction with Holy Spirit is that of *Helper*. We are encouraged by God that His will was never to leave us alone here on the earth. He left us not only a helper, but *The Helper*, Holy Spirit. The word *Helper* means one that helps; especially, a relatively unskilled worker who assists a skilled worker usually by manual labor. There are several words that will help us understand the magnitude of His help in our lives. The first one we will study is the word *Paraclete*. The word *Paraclete* is the Greek word for helper or advocate. It stems from the word *parakletos* which means a person called alongside another to comfort or assist; to aid, to console, comfort, helper or an intercessor. He is forever with us and until the day we leave this earth, His assignment is to be our Helper, or Advocate. The word *Advocate* means one that pleads the cause of another; specifically, one that pleads the cause of another before a tribunal or judicial court; one that defends or maintains a cause or proposal; one that supports or promotes the interests of another.

Holy Spirit is assigned by God to be our advocate in the earth realm. He pleads with God on our behalf and assists Father God in bringing about His perfect will in and through our lives. He helps us to fulfill our God-given purpose, while keeping with God's ultimate plan for humanity. How do we receive this help?

"And I will ask the Father, and He will give you another Helper, to be with you forever, even the Spirit of truth, whom the world cannot receive, because it neither sees Him nor knows Him. You know Him, for He dwells with you and will be in you." John 14:16-17

Jesus was speaking here to His disciples on the Mount of Olives before His ascension. He reveals that the Father will send "another Helper," revealing to them that His assignment was up in the earth, and that another was coming. Though He, Holy Spirit, was already *in* them, He could not be fully activated in their lives, until Jesus Christ left the earth. We know that Jesus commanded them to wait until this Promise, or Help, manifested Himself in their lives.

"But the Helper, the Holy Spirit, whom the Father will send in My name, He will teach you all things, and bring to your remembrance all things that I said to you." John 14:26

Holy Spirit was to be a conduit through which the disciples received reminders of what Jesus taught them. Just as we spoke in an earlier chapter, He not only brings discernment, but also confirmation. If they became weary or distracted, they were able, through Holy Spirit, to encourage themselves in what they had already learned from the Lord. What a beautiful promise to have such a *Helper* in our lives. There is so much we go through on a daily basis, especially in the climate we are now living in today. Chaos, confusion and turmoil surround us on every side, but we are guaranteed help from God to navigate through the turbulent seas of this life. I don't know about you, but that brings great peace to my heart, my mind, my soul and my spirit. Holy Spirit is not only a deposit that guarantees our future redemption with the Lord, but also an assurance of everlasting help from God Himself.

"In Him you also, when you heard the word of truth, the gospel of your salvation, and believed in him, were sealed with the promised Holy Spirit, who is the guarantee of our inheritance until we acquire possession of it, to the praise of his glory." Ephesians 1:13-14

We are sealed! There is no greater peace in knowing that we have the Creator of Heaven and Earth on our side, by our side, as our *Helper*, through the conduit of Holy Spirit. We don't have to do this alone. God does not expect us to feel our way through this life and to face the tests, trials, tribulations and adversities without Him. His Word says He is with us wherever we go, no matter what we do and no matter how far we stray from Him, He is still right there.

"Where can I go from Your Spirit? Or where can I flee from Your presence? If I ascend into heaven, You are there; If I make my bed in hell, behold, You are there. If I take the wings of the morning, And dwell in the uttermost parts of the sea, Even there Your hand shall lead me, And Your right hand shall hold me." Psalm 139:7-10

Oh, He is our *Helper!*

Another aspect of Holy Spirit as our *Paraclete* is through enabling us to live according to the Spirit and to walk and live in the Fruit of the Spirit.

"But the Fruit of the Spirit is love, joy, peace, patience, kindness, goodness, faithfulness, gentleness, self-control; against such things there is no law." Galatians 5:22-23

It is not always easy to walk in the Fruit of the Spirit. There are so many different personalities and spirits we have to deal with on a daily basis, not only in our family, but also in the world, as well as the corporate setting of even our churches. It can be very frustrating and even aggravating, at times, dealing with people. Let's break down each of the fruits of the Spirit to better help us understand, as well as implement, these attributes into our daily lives. We will look at definitions, as well as Biblical meanings of each.

Love
Definition-
1. strong affection for another arising out of kinship or personal ties (maternal love for a child); attraction based on sexual desire: affection and tenderness felt by lovers: affection based on admiration, benevolence, or common interests.

Biblical Meaning-
1. Hebrew: *ahaba-* absolute love, for mankind; God's love toward man
2. Greek: *agape-* love, benevolence, goodwill, esteem; divine love
   Greek: *philadelphia-* brotherly love, love of Christian brethren

"But because the LORD loves you, and because He would keep the oath which He swore to your fathers, the LORD has brought you out with a mighty hand, and redeemed you from the house of bondage, from the hand of Pharaoh king of Egypt." Deuteronomy 7:8

Love, the God kind of love, is unconditional and irrevocable. When we understand how God loves us, it will help us to love one another in the same manner.

Joy
Definition-
1. the emotion evoked by well-being, success, or good fortune or by the prospect of possessing what one desires: delight: the expression or exhibition of such emotion: gaiety
2. a state of happiness or felicity: bliss

Biblical Meaning-
1. Hebrew: *chedvah*- joy, gladness; absolute joy
2. Greek: *agalliasis*- wild joy, ecstatic delight, exultation, exhilaration.

"Then he said to them, "Go your way, eat the fat, drink the sweet, and send portions to those for whom nothing is prepared; for this day is holy to our Lord. Do not sorrow, for the joy of the LORD is your strength." Nehemiah 8:10

The joy of the Lord is not determined by outward circumstances or emotional ups and downs; joy in God stems from Holy Spirit *within* us.

Peace
Definition-
1. a state of tranquility or quiet: as freedom from civil disturbance; a state of security or order within a community provided for by law or custom (a breach of the peace)

2. freedom from disquieting or oppressive thoughts or emotions
3. harmony in personal relations
4. a state or period of mutual concord between governments: a pact or agreement to end hostilities between those who have been at war or in a state of enmity

Biblical Meaning-
1. Hebrew: *shalom*- completeness, soundness, welfare, peace
2. Greek: *eiréneuó*: to bring to peace, to be at peace; living in the condition of God's peace (gift of wholeness, integrity of being).

"That you will do us no harm, since we have not touched you, and since we have done nothing to you but good and have sent you away in peace. You are now the blessed of the LORD." Genesis 26:29

Peace, *shalom*, is probably the most important thing we all seek in our lives. It is not just a temporary fix, but an eternal promise from God. He is Jehovah Shalom, the Prince of Peace.

Patience
Definition-
1. able to remain calm and not become annoyed when waiting for a long time or when dealing with problems or difficult people
2. done in a careful way over a long period of time without hurrying

Biblical Meaning-
1. Hebrew: *arek*- long, slow to anger.
2. Greek: *makrothumia*- patience, long-suffering

"The LORD is gracious and full of compassion, slow to anger and great in mercy." Psalm 145:8

Patience in God is not as the world gives. Just as God is patient with mankind, we, too, ought to be patient with one another. Not everyone grows at the same pace; extend grace and patience to those that may need a little more time, or a little extra push.

Kindness
Definition-
1. a kind deed: favor
2. the quality or state of being kind

Biblical Meaning-
1. Hebrew: *chesed*- goodness, kindness; lovingkindness
2. Greek: *charis*- grace, kindness, as a gift or blessing brought to man by Jesus Christ

"I will worship toward Your holy temple, And praise Your name For Your lovingkindness and Your truth; For You have magnified Your word above all Your name." Psalm 138:2

The world says not to take "kindness for weakness". God revealed His kindness, lovingkindness, through the sacrifice of His Only Son, Jesus Christ. Our kindness toward one another and toward humanity must stem from the kindness we have received from God.

Goodness
Definition-
1. the quality or state of being good
2. the nutritious, flavorful, or beneficial part of something

Biblical meaning-
1. Hebrew: *tub*- fair, gladness, goodness, thing joy, go well with

137

2. Greek: *agathosune*- intrinsic goodness, especially as a personal quality, with stress on the kindly (rather than the righteous) side of goodness.

"Now I myself am confident concerning you, my brethren, that you also are full of goodness, filled with all knowledge, able also to admonish one another." Romans 15:14

Goodness brings something to our lives that cannot be replaced. There is a genuine, warm feeling when you run into a person who exudes the spirit of goodness. It brings the love of Jesus into any situation. May our goodness shine bright for the glory of God.

Faithfulness
Definition-
1. having or showing true and constant support or loyalty
2. deserving trust: keeping your promises or doing what you are supposed to do

Biblical Meaning-
1. Hebrew: *omen*- perfect faithfulness, truth, verity
2. Greek: *pistis*- faith, belief, trust, confidence; fidelity, faithfulness.

"O Lord, You are my God. I will exalt You, I will praise Your name, For You have done wonderful things; Your counsels of old are faithfulness and truth." Isaiah 25:1

It is not so much about our faithfulness to God, but more importantly about His faithfulness to us. As we internalize His great faithfulness, it allows us to serve Him and others with a grateful heart.

Gentleness

Definition-
1. mildness of manners or disposition
2. having or showing a kind and quiet nature : not harsh or violent

Biblical meaning-
1. Hebrew: *anvah-* humility, meekness
2. Greek: *prautés-* consideration, gentleness, humility, meekness

"Let your gentleness be known to all men. The Lord is at hand." Philippians 4:5

A gentle spirit is one that truly expresses the love of God. As we display gentleness, people's hardened hearts are being chiseled away by the precious Holy Spirit.

Self-control

Definition-
1. control over your feelings or actions
2. restraint exercised over one's own impulses, emotions, or desires

Biblical meaning-
1. Hebrew: *tzenuit-* modesty, self-control
2. Greek: *egkrateia-* self-mastery, self-restraint, self-control, continence

"Now for this very reason also, applying all diligence, in your faith supply moral excellence, and in your moral excellence, knowledge, and in your knowledge, self-control, and in your self-control, perseverance, and in your perseverance, godliness, and in your godliness, brotherly kindness, and in your brotherly kindness, love." 2 Peter 1:5-9

To walk in self-mastery or self-control is a weapon in the hand of a Believer. The enemy cannot defeat a Believer that stands upon the Word of God and literally becomes that "living epistle," read by men. He is a strategic tool in the hand of God Almighty!

As we submit to Holy Spirit within, He helps us to walk out the Fruit of the Spirit within our lives. When we live out the Fruit of the Spirit, we "walk by the Spirit" pleasing God and serving others. It is a total life transformation. It is no longer just calling ourselves Christians, it is living the Word of God and allowing it to become an integral part of our everyday lives. When the world begins to see us living what we preach, they will see God in us and glorify Him. He is truly our *Helper!*

Many observations can be made about the Holy Spirit as the *Paraclete* of the Believer. He is personal, powerful, protects, and perseveres. The Spirit convicts, comforts, counsels, and calls us to holy living. As Romans 8:31 teaches, "If God is for us, who can be against us?" It is His utmost desire to walk with us through this life and to lead, guide, direct and instruct us in the ways of God, as well as in His strategic plan for humanity. We have many people that help us throughout our lives, but there is no greater *Helper* we can ever receive than that of Holy Spirit. We do not need to seek "more of God"; He already lives within us. We do not need to go "find God" as believers; He is already within us. We do not need to figure out if God cares about us; He is already with us, caring and guiding to keep us close to Him and His ways. He loves us so very much and says He will never leave us or forsake us; therefore, He sent Holy Spirit to walk with us, talk with us and lead us into God's perfect will for our lives.

He is our *Teacher!* To have someone to walk with us every day and to teach us the ways of God and the way of the Spirit is priceless. We have many teachers throughout our lives, but only that which is done for Christ will last; it is eternal.

"His divine power has granted to us all things that pertain to life and godliness, through the knowledge of Him who called us to His own glory and excellence." 2 Peter 1:3

As we submit to the *Teacher*, Holy Spirit, we are assured that what we have received is from above, not earthly. We can learn many things in the world that will aid us in this life, but to have the precious treasures of heavenly knowledge and wisdom is something that cannot be purchased, or sold.

"As for you, the anointing which you received from Him abides in you, and you have no need for anyone to teach you; but as His anointing teaches you about all things, and is true and is not a lie, and just as it has taught you, you abide in Him." 1 John 2:27

As we remain teachable, Holy Spirit will teach us. Continue to seek His will; continue being a "student of His Word and of His Spirit". He has so much He desires to share with us. Let us be lifetime learners.

"The Spirit leads and guides God's people. "Teach me to do your will, for you are my God; may your good Spirit lead me on level ground" Psalm 143:10

We do not have to walk through this life alone. God has given us His presence, a Teacher, a Helper…His *Holy Spirit!*

Charles H. Spurgeon

"If you do not understand a book by a departed writer you are unable to ask him his meaning, but the Spirit, who inspired Holy Scripture, lives forever, and He delights to open the Word to those who seek His instruction."

"A sinner can no more repent and believe without the Holy Spirit's aid than he can create a world." ~Charles H. Spurgeon

Chapter 10
Holy Spirit:
Comforter/Counselor/Corrector

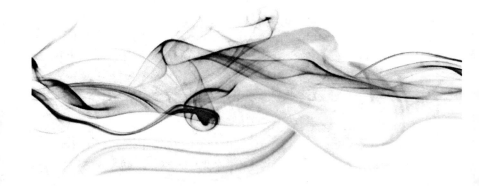

"But the Comforter, which is the Holy Ghost, whom the Father will send in my name, He shall teach you all things, and bring all things to your remembrance, whatsoever I have said unto you." John 14:26, KJV

Our world is plagued by so much hurt, pain, and disappointment; oppression, injustice, and inequality; devastation, destruction and death. As we look out all around us, we see the earth groaning and travailing, as we delve deeper into chaos and confusion. How are we able to stand boldly declaring there is a God in Heaven that loves and cares for us when we see so much turmoil around us? How can we convince a dying world that our God is real and that He is with us when we are visibly shaken ourselves? The next assignment of Holy Spirit we will study is that of the *Comforter*. The word *comforter* means someone who helps you to feel less worried, upset, frightened, etc.; someone who comforts you. The Greek word for comforter is also *Paraclete*, but leans more toward the word Advocate. In this text, the word *Advocate* means a defender, helper, strengthener, as well as comforter. We will deal greater in His role as *Advocate* shortly.

His purpose is much greater than just the "comfort" man can provide to us; Holy Spirit, in His comforting, stands in the gap for our souls as a means to propelling us toward our destiny fulfillment. It is not about making us feel better, but strengthening us to the point of moving us out of our place of stagnancy and into God's perfect will for our lives. He comforts to build us up in His power, releasing us to do great exploits for the Kingdom of God. Let's look at the early church and how they, too, were comforted by Holy Spirit.

"So the church throughout all Judea and Galilee and Samaria enjoyed peace, being built up; and going on in the fear of the Lord and in the comfort of the Holy Spirit, it continued to increase." Acts 9:31

So, we see the multi-faceted purpose of Holy Spirit is greater than just being a "shoulder to cry on" or an "ear to hear" when we need to vent. His purpose in our lives causes great growth and increase. As we submit to the *Comforter*, He is able supply what man cannot. All too often, we place our trust in man and expect them to be all things to us in all seasons of our lives. We become frustrated, bitter, resentful and angry when people don't live up to our expectations of what we think they should be in our lives. If they cannot offer us the consolation we seek, then we are ready to completely cut them out of our lives. I submit to you that many of us are placing expectations upon man when the One we should be seeking for *Comfort* is Holy Spirit. He knows our innermost thoughts and needs; He supplies according to God's riches in glory by Christ Jesus. As we surrender to the Spirit of God within, He is able to meet every need! Set people free from the need to be everything in your life; they cannot offer to you what they do not possess. He is the all-sufficient One! Even Jesus, Himself, understood the need for the *Comforter*, Holy Spirit, in our lives.

"Nevertheless I tell you the truth; It is expedient for you that I go away: for if I go not away, the Comforter will not come unto you; but if I depart, I will send Him unto you." John 16:7, KJV

Though Jesus ascended to Heaven, His Word remains a comfort to those that will believe in Him, while Holy Spirit offers us comfort here in the earth realm by reminding us of His Word and His love. I believe most Christians are frustrated and defeated, because they have refused to acknowledge and accept Holy Spirit as their *Comforter*. He is readily available, but we must receive His promptings within. If we reject Him, then we are left to a very depressed and unfulfilled existence. I have been through a lot over the last fifteen years of my life, even longer. God surely did not promise us a life free from tests, trials and tribulation; in fact, He said to prepare for it. The Word of God says we are in this world, but not of the world. (John 17:14) The world does not stop or completely shift as we become a Christian. In fact, as the days go on, we will see even greater turmoil in our world, but God commands us to be of good cheer, because He has overcome the world.

"These things I have spoken to you, that in Me you may have peace. In the world you will have tribulation; but be of good cheer, I have overcome the world." John 16:33

How are we able to be of good cheer in these turbulent times? By accepting, acknowledging and receiving Holy Spirit into our lives. Holy Spirit is able to comfort us and give us peace, His shalom, in the midst of chaos and confusion. The Spirit-filled life of a Believer in Jesus Christ will reveal to the world who He is and that He desires to give them that very same peace, as well. As you submit to this in your own life, you will be a tremendous light to the world around you. As the world grows darker, we will be salt and light to those that don't know Him. We will be able to comfort them as we are comforted. Even in your families, you will stand as a testament of God's great goodness and love with Him leading you to speak comfort to your loved ones. I am often asked how I can remain so calm and relaxed in the midst of great adversity. I receive many texts, emails and messages asking me to pray for people that are afraid of what is going on in the world, and many of these people are born-again Believers. As I begin to dig deeper, the common denominator in all of their lives is they have yet to experience the fullness of God through Holy Spirit. Either they don't believe in Him, or they are afraid to receive Him. I share my testimony often in the area of Holy Spirit. I knew my life before Him and I can see the evidence of His power within since receiving Him. It is an extreme contrast. Even though I gave my life to Jesus Christ, there was still a very deep void. I lived with great fear and anxiety, even bouts of depression, at times, because I was missing a vital piece of God in my life: *Holy Spirit*. I can testify to you that it was literally like night and day once I accepted His comfort into my life. He completely changed my thinking and provided great consolation as I saw the world falling apart all around me.

"Therefore if there is any consolation in Christ, if any comfort of love, if any fellowship of the Spirit, if any affection and mercy," Philippians 2:1

We can trust that no matter what we encounter in this life, the *Comforter* will always be there for us. As I stated, since I was born-again, I have been through what I could equate to a "living hell on earth". From the age of 14-22, after I lost my father to cancer, I went in a downward spiral. I tried to take my own life and when that didn't work, I lived life in the streets seeking love wherever I could find it. It landed me one night in a wooded area being raped at gunpoint by two men. I cannot say I did not sense or hear the warnings from God all throughout my rebellion. I was His, born-again, yet I was so far away from Him, but not far away enough not to hear that "still small voice". Though I had to endure this dreadful experience, because of my disobedience, I still had the Holy One dwelling on the inside of me. I heard His voice so clearly that night, "Go back home!" This was my wake-up call. He wrapped His loving arms around me and the *Comforter* began to heal, deliver and set me free. He revealed Himself to me as Father God, the Daddy I truly needed after losing my earthly father. I would not find it in a man, only in Him. He swept me off of my feet and cradled me, until I could stand firmly on who I was in Him. My life has never been the same since.

Even after this tremendous ordeal, I faced many other battles throughout my life. I developed cancer not too long after this time. I was told I would never have children after the surgery I went through to remove the cancer. I could have been very angry with God, but there was a peace deep down in my spirit that I was okay, and that He saved me from taking my life, saved me from being raped and murdered, so why would He leave me now? My faith was being formed through each of these tests and trials. Sure enough, I was healed of this cancer and welcomed my first daughter into the world not long after. The *Comforter* was real and alive within me, and I could not explain to others what I was feeling or how I could believe God for inner healing and deliverance, as well as trust Him to "prove to the world" that He was God in my life! I was not only saved, but I was healed! The reports of man were overturned by the *Advocate of Heaven!* Glory to God!

Once again, as I was married and our daughter arrived into the world, and now our son, I was faced with two more episodes of cancer. I cannot explain the peace I had in my spirit. I was not afraid. I trusted fully in Father God that if He had a purpose in saving me from suicide, murder and the first bout of cancer, then He had a plan for this as well. It started with severe migraines to the point where I had to be in a room where absolutely no light could get through. Any hint of light would cause me to cringe in great pain and I would cry until I fell asleep. I would wake up with these migraines. Most people are able to fall asleep and the pain will subside, but this was not the case with me. I was put on the highest dosage of migraine medication, but still, no relief. It became progressively worse where my sight began to be affected. I would stand in church during Worship and everything began to become blurry. I experienced what some call "eye floaters". It was like I was looking into a kaleidoscope. I would sit down, close my eyes, and just worship my Abba Father. This, coupled with severe migraines, almost completely debilitated me. Doctors could not figure out why I was experiencing this. It progressed into severe muscle dysfunction. The only way I can explain it is as if someone was inside of me twisting my muscles; wringing them out as if they were a towel full of water. It got to a point where I could not even move. This took place over a period of about six months. I lay in my bed one night in excruciating pain and I cried out to God to heal me...and that He did! I was supernaturally healed that night, and I have not experienced anything of this sort again.

> "But He was wounded for our transgressions, He was bruised for our iniquities; the chastisement for our peace was upon Him, And by His stripes we are healed." Isaiah 53:5

Again, my faith was being strengthened in ways unimaginable. I did not once question why this was happening to me. It was truly supernatural. Not only supernatural healing, but supernatural faith and trust in God were being formed in my life. I delved into the Word of God and prayer unlike any other time since I was saved at twelve years old. I began to pray in ways I never had before and great insight and revelation began to be opened up to me during prayer. I was prophesied over not too longer after this that God was calling me as an intercessor. The more I interceded, the less I would pray for myself. I just knew in my spirit that God would take care of me and be my *Comforter*.

After about a year, I began to develop mini tumors in several places on my body, mostly on my head and face. Being in Germany, the military hospital could not figure out what was causing this. I was sent to a German hospital where every test known to man was done upon me. I felt like I was in some sort of Sci-Fi movie in the basement of this German hospital. They could not find out the root of these growths, tumors, on my skin. There was one at the base of my forehead between my eyes, right at the edge of the bridge of my nose. It began to grow exponentially. I, thinking it was just acne or something similar, popped it and the fluid leaked all the way through my face. My face became so enlarged to the point that my eyes were almost completely shut due to the swelling. I gave up on the doctors and went to the Chief Physician, Jesus Christ! I went to my pastors while we were in Germany and they laid hands on me and declared God's healing over my body and I was healed, once again, supernaturally.

"Now a woman, having a flow of blood for twelve years, who had spent all her livelihood on physicians and could not be healed by any, came from behind and touched the border of His garment. And immediately her flow of blood stopped. And Jesus said, "Who touched Me?" Luke 8:43-45a

I truly felt like this woman. I was tired of doctors and so many different "guesses" at what was wrong with me. Several encouraged me to begin chemotherapy, even though they couldn't put a "name" to what I had. I realized that even if man could put a name on it, I did not have to accept their report, but the report of the Lord. And His report is that we *were healed!* The comfort of His Word and from the *Comforter* Himself, Holy Spirit, I was convinced that there was a greater purpose at work in my life through all of these instances of sickness and disease. Not that God sends it, but He allowed it to develop my faith and trust in Him. I also know the call on my life has been a personal assignment of the devil himself. As I look back over my life, I see the multiple attempts to steal, kill and destroy my very existence. Many times, I have felt like Job, but

I understand that the enemy can do nothing to me that God has not allowed. In knowing this, it has allowed me to grow even closer to Daddy God. Through it all, it has given me a faith for miraculous healing. God has brought many people into my life in need of physical healing. He has allowed me to minister not only my testimony, but used my faith to pray for, as well as lay hands on the sick and they have recovered. I refuse to believe that our Lord died on the Cross for our sins, as well as our sickness and disease, in vain. I have had multiple attacks on my body over my lifetime, even recently, but I stand upon the Word of God and put my trust in the One who comforts me. He has not failed me yet, and He won't.

"God is not a man, that He should lie, Nor a son of man, that He should repent. Has He said, and will He not do? Or has He spoken, and will He not make it good?" Numbers 23:19

Rest in this truth. Be comforted in knowing that He holds the world together with His Word; and at His Word it will be judged. He knows the very number of hairs upon our heads and holds time and space within His hand. He knows the time of our birth and the time of our death. Surrender yourself to His will and submit to the leading of Holy Spirit within. This journey called life is an amazing and exciting experience if we allow Holy Spirit to guide us, lead us and instruct us. When we get to the place of seeing Him as the *Comforter*, we can let go and step out into the deep waters to see Him in ways we have never witnessed.

He not only comforts us in times of sickness and disease, but He is also the *Comforter* sent to walk with us during our process of preparation towards the call of God upon our lives. We know the enemy wants to destroy us before we even realize what the call is, but when we do begin to walk towards it or walk in it, he knows his kingdom, the kingdom of darkness, is about to be pulled up and rooted out. Every person in the Word of God that was being prepared for their call was led by Holy Spirit either into a pit, a cave, a desert or a wilderness. It is in these places where we are stripped of all we trust in, except for Him. These crucial seasons are very lonely and dry and everything within us is tested. But again, as we put our trust in God, and submit to the process, Holy Spirit will endow us with a peace and comfort that is unexplainable. It is in these necessary times where we grow to know the *Comforter* of our souls.

In my latest book *The Wilderness*[ix], I reveal the process God took me through in releasing me into my calling. It was a very difficult journey, but a very necessary one. He broke me, humbled me, purged me, molded me, shaped me, and ultimately, prepared me to be His voice to the Church. I was taught, trained, empowered, encouraged and equipped by Holy Spirit Himself. This kind of preparation can only come by way of Holy Spirit. No man is able to complete this type of work in the life of an individual. You will have pastors, spiritual leaders, mentors, and friends, even family that are able to comfort and encourage you to fight the good fight of faith, but only God, through Holy Spirit, can completely transform your life in this way. From Moses to Elijah, David to Job and most importantly our Lord and Savior, Jesus Christ, all were led into their time of testing.

"Then Jesus was led up by the Spirit into the wilderness to be tempted by the devil." Matthew 4:1

Why would God allow Jesus to one, be led into the wilderness and two, be tempted by the devil if He was God? He wanted us to understand not only the ways of the enemy, but also to reveal the comfort and "keeping power" of Holy Spirit to guard us, protect us and yes, comfort us through the darkest seasons of our lives. With all that I faced during my wilderness seasons, I should have walked completely away from God, let alone the church, but I had a precious gift that kept me...the *Comforter*, Holy Spirit. As the opening scripture states, He will bring all things to our remembrance. (John 14:26) He reminded me of God's faithfulness over my life. He took me back and showed me how He saved me, healed me, delivered me and kept me. He brought the Word of God back to my heart each and every time I needed to encourage myself or speak life over my situations. He was there for me, and is still here for me every step of the way. He is faithful to those that will put their full trust in Him. He truly comforts the comfortless. Oftentimes, in fact, the majority of the time, we will want to outright give up on this walk with God. It is easy by no means whatsoever. This is truly a walk of sacrifice, surrender, submission and selflessness. It is literally dying to ourselves, laying down our lives for the cause of Christ. I am confident that we would not be able to do this without the aid of the *Comforter*, Holy Spirit.

As we come out of these wilderness seasons and pass the testing of God, He is able to release us into His promise over our lives. Holy Spirit, the *Comforter*, is with us every step of the way. It is absolutely encouraging to know that He walks with us through these seasons. Let's take a look at the process Jesus was taken through and how the *Comforter*, Holy Spirit, was with Him the entire time.

1. **Proclamation**
   "When He had been baptized, Jesus came up immediately from the water; and behold, the heavens were opened to Him, and He saw the Spirit of God descending like a dove and alighting upon Him. And suddenly a voice came from heaven, saying, "This is My beloved Son, in whom I am well pleased." Matthew 3: 16-17

2. **Process**
   "Then Jesus was led up by the Spirit into the wilderness to be tempted by the devil." Matthew 4:1

3. **Preparation**
   "And Jesus went about all Galilee, teaching in their synagogues, preaching the gospel of the kingdom, and healing

all kinds of sickness and all kinds of disease among the people." Matthew 4:23

4. **Promise**
   "And Jesus came and spoke to them, saying, "All authority has been given to Me in heaven and on earth. Go therefore and make disciples of all the nations, baptizing them in the name of the Father and of the Son and of the Holy Spirit, teaching them to observe all things that I have commanded you; and lo, I am with you always, even to the end of the age." Amen." Matthew 28:18-20

If Jesus is our example, which He absolutely is, then we need to learn to receive all that He has to offer us, including His great comfort, as we walk through the *not so easy* seasons of our lives. What a joy it is to know we are not alone on this journey. Thanks be to God who gives us the victory through our Lord and Savior Jesus Christ, and who provides His precious Spirit, the *Comforter*, to encourage, exhort and equip us to walk in His divine purpose for our lives. Receive His comfort today!

"My little children, I am writing these things to you so that you may not sin And if anyone sins, we have an Advocate with the Father, Jesus Christ the righteous;" 1 John 2:1

In the same way Holy Spirit is our *Comforter*, He reveals Himself as our *Counselor*. Though Jesus ascended to Heaven, He remains an advocate for the Believer at the right hand of the Father in the spiritual realm, while Holy Spirit offers us advocacy, or comfort, here in the earth realm. I believe most Christians are frustrated and defeated, because they have refused to acknowledge and accept Holy Spirit as their *Advocate*. He is readily available, but we must receive His promptings within. The Hebrew word for advocate is *sahed*, or witness. The word *counselor* is defined as a person who provides advice as a job; a person who counsels people. The Greek word for counselor is *sumboulos*, which means a consultant, formal advisor or counselor. All of these terms, Biblically speaking, represent the idea of a courtroom-like position; He stands as a lawyer, an advocate, or a counselor on our behalf in the earth. As we submit our lives to Jesus Christ, Holy Spirit comes immediately and "sets up residence" within us. His assignment is activated upon salvation. He stands in defense of what is His; we are now children of God.

It is God's desire to counsel His people through the Word of God, but also through Holy Spirit. There are many times where we don't have the Word readily available in our hands, but as we hide it in our hearts, Holy Spirit is able to bring back to our remembrance all things pertaining to the Word for each of our life situations. Holy Spirit shines light upon, or illuminates our circumstances and provides wise counsel for us to walk it out for the glory of Father God. It is easy for us to just do what seems right, but not everything that is considered "good" is God. John Bevere in his book "Good or God? Why Good Without God Isn't Enough,"[x] states:

"These days the terms good and God seem synonymous. We believe what's generally accepted as good must be in line with God's will. Generosity, humility, justice—good. Selfishness, arrogance, cruelty—evil. The distinction seems pretty straightforward. But is that all there is to it? If good is so obvious, why does the Bible say that we need discernment to recognize it?"

Holy Spirit, being our *Counselor*, provides us with the discernment necessary to determine what our own will is and what the will of God is. So many believers, not being filled with Holy Spirit, or not accessing His power within, make many decisions based upon feelings, opportunities, and many times, their flesh. I heard a pastor preach one time and he encouraged us to never turn down an opportunity. He stated that every opportunity could be grasped and used for our good; that we should not turn down doors that are clearly wide open for us. My spirit was grieved, because I understood this concept that "not everything good is God". We know the temptation of Jesus in the wilderness where Satan offered Him the kingdoms of this world. If we are not seeking the counsel of Holy Spirit, we can easily walk through doors that God did not open for us. In doing so, we open the door to carnal and worldly spirits that if not cast out quickly; can lead to deep strongholds in our lives. It is pertinent to receive our *Counselor* sent by God to lead us, guide us, direct us and walk us through this life. It is foolish not accept such a precious gift!

"But solid food belongs to those who are of full age, that is, those who by reason of use have their senses exercised to discern both good and evil." Hebrews 5:14

Many of us pray and ask God to give us clear and precise answers and direction in our lives. Whether we are seeking Him for a spouse, trying to decide to go to college or start a business, when to have children, or even where spiritually to plant our family, there are specific seasons each of us is predestined to do so, and Holy Spirit will lead us if we allow Him. Not all of us have taken this route early on in our lives. Many of us did not receive Holy Spirit until later on in life; some, never. So, we are left to our own devices to determine what is good for us and for our families, but we don't always make the right decisions, and we're left having to go back and do it over. God wants us to receive Him early on, so that we don't have to go through so many struggles in our lives. Not saying we won't, because sometimes detours are a part of His plan, but we know when we are "circling the wilderness" just as the children of Israel did, because of their disobedience.

Holy Spirit is the mind and heart of God. He relays God's intent for mankind. His multiplicity of attribute provides the Believer with all they need to navigate through this earthly life and to fulfill the call of God upon their lives. Open your heart today and receive the *Counselor*, Holy Spirit.

The final attribute we will discuss is that of *Corrector*. The word *correct* is defined as to punish (as a child) with a view to reforming or improving; to point out usually for amendment the errors or faults of. The Hebrew word for "correct" is *musar*, meaning discipline, chastening, or correction; instruction, chastisement, or reproof. God's way of correction never sets out to condemn, but always points to His love for us. Holy Spirit will correct us, so we can get back on the right path. He does not want us to fail; His desire is for us to always be prosperous in every area of our lives. But He will never allow us to have everything earthly and lose the most precious gift in our lives...eternal life with Him. Correction is a tool in the hand of God through Holy Spirit that can completely transform us into His image and likeness. If we are to call ourselves followers of Jesus Christ, then there is much we need to shed of our old nature, in order to walk as new creatures. We cannot effectively walk in the light and darkness at the same time and expect God to be with us. If we are going to live this life, then we are going to have to die daily to self, our flesh, so that Holy Spirit can live within us unhindered, in freedom.

So many of us that call ourselves Christians, or followers of Christ, have a very hard time with correction. No one likes to be corrected; it does not feel good and many times, if we are not submitted to Holy Spirit within, our flesh will surely rise up in opposition to any form of correction, no matter who it is sent through. It is just like with our children, they don't like to receive the correction and discipline of their parents, but we know, as parents, if we do not provide the discipline, then we are ultimately setting them up for failure. The Word of God says in Hebrews 12:6-11:

> "For whom the Lord loves He chastens, And scourges every son whom He receives." If you endure chastening, God deals with you as with sons; for what son is there whom a father does not chasten? But if you are without chastening, of which all have become partakers, then you are illegitimate and not

sons. Furthermore, we have had human fathers who corrected us, and we paid them respect. Shall we not much more readily be in subjection to the Father of spirits and live? For they indeed for a few days chastened us as seemed best to them, but He for our profit, that we may be partakers of His holiness. Now no chastening seems to be joyful for the present, but painful; nevertheless, afterward it yields the peaceable fruit of righteousness to those who have been trained by it."

Let's look at a few more instances in Scripture that lend credibility to the correction of the Lord:

"My son, do not despise the chastening of the Lord, Nor detest His correction; For whom the Lord loves He corrects, Just as a father the son in whom he delights." Proverbs 3:12

"Behold, happy is the man whom God corrects; Therefore do not despise the chastening of the Almighty." Job 5:17

See, the ultimate goal is training and equipping us to be partakers of His holiness, to walk in righteousness before Him and before mankind. Through each of these scriptures, we are affirmed of His love for us in doing so. The sad reality is the state of the church today has all but abandoned the correction, chastisement, discipline and yes, rebuke of our Lord. We have trampled upon our Lord and sought out others to excuse our disobedience, instead of holding us accountable to it. Outright sin in the church, as well as the pulpit, is celebrated as "the grace of God". Sin is no longer preached about in the pulpit, because we are worried about offending people. We don't want people to leave the church, so we water down the Gospel and begin teaching false doctrines to keep the seats filled. What we are doing is rebelling against the Word of God and Holy Spirit. The Word of God is clear on correction, as well as rebuke. It is a necessary tool not only to provide order in the local congregation, but to reinstate the reverence of the Lord in the heart of the

Believer. There is almost a non-existence of reverential fear of the Lord in today's church.

"Those who are sinning rebuke in the presence of all, that the rest also may fear." 1 Timothy 5:20

If we took this Word we call our manual to Christ likeness and lived it, instead of just preaching it, things would be very different in the church today. We have pastors and spiritual leaders in outright sin and disobedience being hailed as trailblazers of 'the grace of God'. In many instances, there is no correction at all. There is no accountability and they are allowed to continue preaching as if nothing ever happened? When there is no accountability in the pulpit, those in the "pews" take this as an all out "get out of jail free pass" and feel if their pastor does not have to be held accountable, neither do they. It is as the scripture above states, when we openly rebuke the sin in the presence of all, the fear of the Lord comes upon us and causes us to evaluate the sin in our own lives and to overcome it through His Word and Holy Spirit.

Correction is very similar to the word reproof, which implies and often kindly intent to correct a fault. Correction, if not received in humility, can and will lead to rebuke. The word *rebuke* is defined as expressing sharp disapproval or criticism of (someone) because of their behavior or actions. This is similar to the Biblical definition, yet rebuke by God is not meant to criticize, but correct and turn us back to Him. The Greek word is *epitimao*, meaning to reprimand; strongly warn; restrain.

"As many as I love, I rebuke and chasten. Therefore be zealous and repent." Revelation 3:19

Again, we see the love of Father God toward us, not punishment or a critical spirit, but one that wholeheartedly desires for His children to walk in His Truth and in His Spirit. If we desire to be used by God and to walk out our purpose here on earth, we must submit ourselves to His correction, chastisement and yes, His rebuke, if necessary. He equates the receiving of rebuke as wisdom, and those that refuse it are considered fools.

"It is better to hear the rebuke of the wise, Than for a man to hear the song of fools." Ecclesiastes 7:5

"A wise son heeds his father's instruction, But a scoffer does not listen to rebuke." Proverbs 13:1

Let us grow deeper in spiritual maturity and become the sons God is calling us to be in the Kingdom. Holy Spirit, the *Corrector*, if we allow Him, is able to touch upon places within our lives that are hidden; that need to come towards the light, so He is able to expose it and deliver us in the process. As followers of Christ, we need to be keenly aware of the enemy's deceptive nature. He desires to keep us in darkness; hiding things in our lives that God wants to shine light upon. Holy Spirit will reveal things in our lives that keep us from the fullness of Father God. He will gently speak to us to get that thing right and to put the enemy under our feet, but when we refuse and reject that "still small voice," the light grows dimmer within us and can be extinguished. The longer we neglect Holy Spirit's promptings, the more we allow the door open for the spirit of error.

Ananias and Sapphira were a very wealthy couple that chose to sell all they had to follow the disciples of Jesus Christ. They came, along with many others, and offered their entire life savings for the furthering of the Gospel; yet, they held back a portion for themselves and buried it. Holy Spirit revealed to Peter that they had lied to him and to God and now; they would suffer the consequences of their lies.

"But Peter said, "Ananias, why has Satan filled your heart to lie to the Holy Spirit, and to keep back some of the price of the land?" Acts 5:3

The excuse of Ananias was they had given much more than anyone and that what they had given was sufficient enough, but that is not what they exclaimed upon entering the camp; they proclaimed before God and man that they had sold everything to spread the Gospel of Jesus Christ. We must be aware of deception and the consequences of it. Once we offer one lie, we have to keep lying, in order to keep the previous hidden. This is probably one of the greatest ways in which Satan tricks people today, as well as in previous generations. He can keep us in bondage, as long as he has "evidence" on us. Let's look at several ways in which we can offend the Spirit of God, so we will not make the same mistake Ananias and Sapphira made, as well as many others throughout history.

There is probably no greater fear Believers have than to offend Holy Spirit. We are taught many things throughout our walk with the Lord, but as many of us know, this is one area that is the most consequential to our lives in Christ Jesus. Throughout this entire book, we are reminded that once we receive Jesus Christ as our Lord and Savior, Holy Spirit is immediately activated in our lives. After Pentecost, Holy Spirit was available and moving throughout the earth in the hearts of mankind. Holy Spirit was confirming the Truth that Jesus Christ was, and is, the Son of the Living God. Even after this, many still refused to believe it. Let's look at offenses committed by both believer and unbeliever.

a) Resisting Holy Spirit.
"You men who are stiff-necked and uncircumcised in heart and ears are always resisting the Holy Spirit." Acts 7:51

Mankind is wooed daily by Holy Spirit. He is relentless in His approach to draw God's people to the saving knowledge of Jesus Christ. He goes above and beyond to confirm through many different situations and people that Jesus is, indeed, the Son of the Living God and our Savior. Yet, we continue to refuse the truth and then resist the conviction of Holy Spirit. For some, it is an outright refusal to believe; we want to do what we want without consequence or accountability. We believe as we reject Him as Lord and Savior, we are not accountable, but this is a lie from the pit of hell. When Holy Spirit moves upon our hearts and we sense it, but choose, at that moment, to reject it, we are in error. Many believe they can live their lives any way they choose and then, when they are ready, ask Him into their lives. Sadly, all too often, this never occurs, either because of untimely departure from this life, or we obtain too much "stuff" that we have no need for God. But for others, life has dealt them hard blows where they find it extremely difficult to believe that God could allow such hurt, pain and disappointment. Many see great destruction and devastation at a very early age, including abuse of every kind: physical, mental, emotional and yes, sexual. It is very difficult to turn all of that over to God to heal them, but yet, He still comforts the unbeliever's heart and shows them the Truth of Jesus Christ. Either way, Holy Spirit will continue to reveal to them God's sovereignty, but they choose to resist Him. Choose today to respond to that inner witness, the knower...*Holy Spirit.*

b) Insulting Holy Spirit.
"How much worse punishment, do you think, will be deserved by the one who has . . . outraged the Spirit of grace?" Hebrews 10:29

Holy Spirit's role in the life of a Believer has many characteristics, as we saw in previous chapters. One such characteristic, or attribute, is that of illumination. Holy Spirit will "bring to light" in the heart of the Believer the truth of who Jesus is; His deity. Many unbelievers believe in "God," "a god," or a "higher power," yet refuse to acknowledge that Jesus died on the Cross, rose from the dead and is seated at the right hand of Father God. They see Him as an ordinary man that died on a cross. When Holy Spirit reveals the truth of His deity and we deny it, we subsequently insult the "Spirit of grace," or Holy Spirit. God sends us many confirmations, through people and situations, to come to Him. Some will outright criticize the work of Holy Spirit and deny its power. In all these things, we are resisting Holy Spirit.

c) Blaspheming the Holy Spirit.

"And whoever shall speak a word against the Son of Man, it shall be forgiven him; but whoever shall speak against the Holy Spirit, it shall not be forgiven him, either in this age, or in the age to come." Matthew 12:32

Blasphemy is considered the greatest sin; the unpardonable sin, according to the Word of God. It is the culmination of resisting, insulting and subsequently calling Holy Spirit a liar. When we continually reject the leading of Holy Spirit, we are led into great rebellion against God. These people's hearts are ultimately hardened toward God and the atonement of our sins through Jesus Christ. Not to mention refusing to hear the voice of Holy Spirit. In essence, they reject the triune Godhead of Father, Son and Holy Spirit.

d) Grieving the Spirit.

"And do not grieve the Holy Spirit of God, by whom you were sealed for the day of redemption. Let all bitterness, wrath, anger, clamor, and evil speaking be put away from you, with all malice." Ephesians: 30-31

Holy Spirit is the most sensitive person of the Godhead. To grieve means to make sad or sorrowful. It is the word used to describe the experience of Christ in the Garden of Gethsemane. Jesus was not able to endure the testing of this crucial place without the aid of Holy Spirit. When we allow these things, bitterness, wrath, anger or evil speaking, to have reign in our hearts, we grieve Holy Spirit. The Word of God tells us to crucify the deeds of the flesh and walk in the Spirit. It grieves the heart of God, and Holy Spirit, when a born-again Believer walks carnally and according to the world. Put these things away from you and choose to walk according to the Spirit of God.

e) Lying to Holy Spirit.

"But Peter said, "Ananias, why has Satan filled your heart to lie to the Holy Spirit and keep back part of the price of the land for yourself? While it remained, was it not your own? And after it was sold, was it not in your own control? Why have you conceived this thing in your heart? You have not lied to men but to God." Acts 5:3-4

Many of us are quick to say we have surrendered fully to the Lord, yet hold back just as Ananias did. We may not hold back financially as he did, but compromise our faith in other ways, while portraying on the outside that we are completely sold out to God. This is lying to Holy Spirit. Holy Spirit knows everything concerning us and although we can try, we cannot deceive the Spirit of God. In doing so, we are bringing great devastation upon our lives. Choose to walk wholeheartedly with God, even in the hard times. He is not calling us to be perfect; He only desires we come to Him when we have fallen. Be real with God today.

f) Quenching the Spirit.
"Do not quench not the Spirit." 1 Thessalonians 5:19

Quenching the Spirit is likened to putting out a fire. Holy Spirit is the fire of God within the Believer's life. As Holy Spirit manifests in our lives, God speaks to us very specific instructions, direction and strategies. If we refuse His voice, we quench not only the Spirit in our hearts, but also in the hearts of others. People are watching us; many look to us as God begins to manifest through Holy Spirit in our lives. In our disobedience to the leading of the Spirit, others can become discouraged and lose faith in God. We can also develop a critical spirit when it comes to prophecy, the preaching of the Word or even the testimonies of other Believers. In doing so, we quench Holy Spirit and the fire of God becomes extinguished within our lives and the lives of others. Surrender to His leading and trust God that He knows what is best for our lives.

Let us grow closer daily in His presence. Let Him wash us in His Truth. As we submit to His Spirit within, we are fashioned to think, walk, talk and move in heavenly places with Father God.

"Therefore, brethren, having boldness to enter the Holiest by the blood of Jesus, by a new and living way which He consecrated for us, through the veil, that is, His flesh, and having a High Priest over the house of God, let us draw near with a true heart in full assurance of faith, having our hearts sprinkled from an evil conscience and our bodies washed with pure water." Hebrews 10:19-22

He is our *Comforter*, our *Counselor*, our *Corrector* and He is sent to help us stay the course, to run our race and to receive the Victory through our Lord and Savior, Jesus Christ. He is *Holy Spirit!*

William Seymour

"The first step in seeing baptism with the Holy Ghost, is to have a clear knowledge of the new birth in our souls, which is the first work of grace and brings everlasting life to our souls."

"God is calling His people to true holiness in these days."
~*William Seymour*

Chapter 11

Holy Spirit:
Intercessor/Revealer

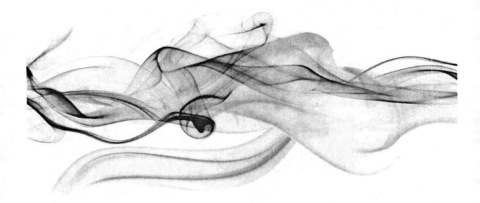

"And in the same way the Spirit also helps our weakness; for we do not know how to pray as we should, but the Spirit Himself intercedes for us with groanings too deep for words." Romans 8:26

God sought out a man in the earth that would stand in the gap for His people, an intercessor, so He did not have to destroy the land, but the Word says He found not one, so He stretched forth His own arm, His Son Jesus Christ, and brought salvation to mankind. (Isaiah 59:16) How devastating to know that not one man was willing to sacrifice his life in intercession to pray on behalf of the world. God did not ask someone to lay down his life, physically, for the land; He simply asked, "Will someone just pray?" I cannot fathom a world, or an era, where no one had a heart to pray? I can only imagine what this time in history looked like. What grief God must have had that out of His entire Creation, not one had His heart for mankind. But there was One…His Son, Jesus Christ. He alone was the hedge, the wall, and the arm extended out toward humanity. He stood in the gap between Heaven and Earth. He was the bridge connecting us to eternity. So who greater to be called our Intercessor, the One seated on the right hand of Father God making intercession for the saints.

> "Who shall bring a charge against God's elect? It is God who justifies. Who is he who condemns? It is Christ who died, and furthermore is also risen, who is even at the right hand of God, who also makes intercession for us." Romans 8: 33-34

With Jesus standing in the gap for humanity, is there even a need for us to continue to intercede? If we feel Jesus is taking care of it all, then we can just sit back and receive, right? Wrong. Intercession in the earth realm after Jesus' ascension has more to do with the heart of man than the sovereignty of our Lord. It also opens the door to intimacy and partnership with Father God and His Creation. I believe it was His initial plan for mankind; to walk in complete partnership in the earth realm. As I began to learn what intercession was, my prayer life, my walk with God, my faith in Him, as well as my love for mankind began to grow tremendously. After a while, I stopped praying for myself and my needs, and began to shift my thoughts, prayers and yes, intercession outward. God began to give me His heart for humanity. As you receive the revelation of intercession, the magnitude of its impact in the earth realm, you will never be, or see, the same again!

> "I exhort therefore, that, first of all, supplications, prayers, intercessions, [and] giving of thanks, be made for all men;' 1 Timothy 2:1

For the Believer to stand in the gap in intercession in the earth, we are partnering with the Spirit of God, Holy Spirit. We have the Spirit within and He will lead us as to who and what to pray/intercede for. It is not in our "normal" makeup to intercede on behalf of others. Yes, when we know there is a tragedy or that someone is struggling in an area, we will pray for them, but there is another level of prayer where God, through Holy Spirit, will place someone on your heart either by bringing them to your mind for no apparent reason or through dreams and visions. This is markedly different from a "prayer request;" this is a divine unction orchestrated by God Himself through the vein of Holy Spirit. He "stands in the gap" between God and man, relaying the heart of the Father for humanity. We partner with Holy Spirit, as He imparts the unknown, the hidden, and we make up the "breach" for individuals and situations.

Intercession is defined as the action of intervening on behalf of another; mediation, arbitration, or negotiation. The Hebrew word for intercession is *paga*, meaning come between, cause to entreat, fall upon, make intercession, intercessor, entreat; to attack, approach, strike or encounter. This biblical meaning hits the target on God's heart for intercession. It connotes a war term. Intercession is doing battle in the spiritual realm on behalf of earthly outcomes. These are not just mere words I am speaking; I have lived the life of an intercessor for over fifteen years and have seen and heard many calls to intercession for people and situations all over the world. I know it is nothing but the hand of God, as I would never, in my own capacity, intercede like I have by the leading of Holy Spirit. I have spent many long nights in travailing intercession for people and situations. Please listen to no one that tells you spiritual warfare is not a New Testament necessity, or that we are not called to battle spiritually in the earth realm. I have heard many pastors and believers alike that hold this theory heavily, but it is not Biblical.

"Finally, my brethren, be strong in the Lord and in the power of His might. Put on the whole armor of God, that you may be able to stand against the wiles of the devil. For we do not wrestle against flesh and blood, but against principalities, against powers, against the rulers of the darkness of this age, against spiritual hosts of wickedness in the heavenly places." Ephesians 6:10-12

We are in a war for our souls, and the souls of mankind. This is not a physical fight, but a spiritual one, so we war with spiritual weapons. If we are not taught how to war spiritually, when we are confronted with spiritual attacks, then we are left wide open for the enemy's onslaught. At the writing of this very chapter, I was in deep intercession all night long. I had been covering a team of missionaries ministering in Romania and Sweden, as well as a group of Believers in Switzerland. The breakthrough and deliverance taking place with these missionaries is nothing short of the hand of God. Muslims were giving their lives to Jesus and going back home to get their families to bring them to these gatherings. Healing, deliverance and salvations are springing up in this Persian community.

As I joyfully entered into intercession for both of these groups, rejoicing and giving God thanks for His faithfulness, the tone of intercession shifted. I was now on my face heavily weeping and praying in the Spirit for hours. After I felt the burden lift, I went to bed. Within minutes of closing my eyes, I sensed a heavy darkness around me. I opened up my eyes and my room did not look familiar (I have experienced this more times than I can count), so I knew what I was facing here. I began to speak the Word out of my mouth and prayed in the Spirit as well. I lay back down and it happened again, but this time, I was experiencing a spiritual attack on my body. I felt my head starting to spin and I felt great pressure and my breathing was being affected. I got up and went into my living room and opened up the Word and God took me straight to Ephesians. I read the entire book and meditated upon it until the peace of God blanketed me. By this time, it was 6:00am; I had been up all night in intercession and yes, spiritual warfare.

"Therefore take up the whole armor of God, that you may be able to withstand in the evil day, and having done all, to stand. Stand therefore, having girded your waist with truth, having put on the breastplate of righteousness, and having shod your feet with the preparation of the gospel of peace; above all, taking the shield of faith with which you will be able to quench all the fiery darts of the wicked one." Ephesians 6:13-16

I believe those that criticize this part of a Believer's walk assume it is this wild and crazy screaming session, throwing oil around and rebuking the devil. No, it is recognition of an attack and simply taking authority over it through prayer, intercession and the Word of God. I firmly believe if we are doing the will of God, we are going to face these kinds of spiritual attacks. The enemy does not touch what is not a threat to his kingdom. And as we partner with Holy Spirit, the Spirit of Intercession, our *Intercessor*, our war strategist; He is able to give us strategic insight, illumination and revelation from the heart of Father God for each and every situation we encounter.

"And He who searches the hearts knows what the mind of the Spirit is, because He intercedes for the saints according to the will of God." Romans 8:27

Intercession is Spirit-led. Sure, we can choose to stand in the gap for people and declare God's promise over their lives, and stay in that vein, until we see breakthrough. But there are times when we are nowhere in the mindset of interceding for someone, yet, Holy Spirit will lay them on our hearts or reveal a situation that needs to be covered and will give us specific instructions on how to do so effectively. I believe this can be considered prophetic intercession where a situation is not previously known and is opened up to us right at the moment of intercession. Holy Spirit opens the eyes and ears of our spirit and downloads heavenly insight and revelation. Prophetic intercession is a gateway into the spiritual realm that provides us access, keys, to the unlocking of "chains" and "prison doors" in individual lives and over nations to set the captives free. The level at which you offer yourself in intercession, will reveal the "ranks" of those sent to stop you from doing so. Daniel was notified of this kind of warfare by the angel Gabriel that revealed he was being withstood by the "Prince of Persia" (Daniel 10). Keep yourselves clothed in His armor, the armor of God and He will use you to carry out His perfect plan in the earth realm.

The word *revelation* means a surprising and previously unknown fact, especially one that is made known in a dramatic way; the divine or supernatural disclosure to humans of something relating to human existence or the world. The Greek word for revelation is *apokalupsis*, which means an unveiling, uncovering, revealing; appearing, coming, manifestation or revelation. What a privilege and an honor that God would reveal to mere man His plans and purposes and that we can, as I stated earlier, partner with Him to carry out His will in the earth realm. After fifteen or so years, it is still mind-blowing to me that the Creator of the Universe, Almighty God, would communicate with us. He loves us so very much!

As God reveals Himself through Holy Spirit, our spirits connect with the Spirit of God. I hear so often, not from the world, but from carnal Christians that people are so 'heavenly minded that they are no earthly good,' or that people are "too spiritual". I used to get really offended when I heard this, as I knew this was a place of true intimacy and fellowship with Father God through Holy Spirit. It is a very special and precious place for any Believer to live in, and we are empowered through Holy Spirit to be witnesses in this dark world, so I was confused as to why many Christians were "offended" by this place? I realized very early on that it was not necessarily 'my' offense, but the conviction of others that did not have this kind of fellowship with God through Holy Spirit. Until you have been in this place with God, you cannot and will not understand it. It is available to all, but few actually take advantage of true, authentic relationship with Father God.

"And it is the Spirit who bears witness, because the Spirit is the truth." 1 John 5:6

We want to be saved and to live eternally with Father God, yet we refuse and reject His power and authority in the earth realm through Holy Spirit. So many Believers are frustrated and are quick to say that prayer does not work; that God does not hear us and He is not communicating with mankind. I am here to tell you that I am a living witness of the power of God through Holy Spirit. God is still speaking and He is still answering the prayers of His people! The problem most Believers experience is when we don't acknowledge Holy Spirit, the *Revealer*, in our lives; our prayers are self-motivated and not Christ-centered. As we submit and surrender our lives to Jesus Christ, His will is formed within us. Our lives are no longer our own. We are called to die daily to ourselves and to take upon His life, His likeness and His will. As we pray and intercede, the Spirit of God within, the *Revealer*, Holy Spirit...begins to reveal the heart and mind of God to us. As the above scripture states, the Spirit bears witness, because the Spirit is Truth. We can trust Holy Spirit, because He is the Spirit of Truth.

"He will glorify Me, for He will take of Mine and will disclose it to you." John 16:14

He glorifies Father God as He discloses, or reveals, God's heart to us, His people. He is truly a gift to us. The very answers we are seeking lie within the conduit of the *Revealer*, Holy Spirit. He reveals to us the wisdom of God for our situations. I don't understand how Believers make it in this life without Him? I need Him every second of every day, as I pray without ceasing and seek God in every area of my life.

"For to us God revealed them through the Spirit; for the Spirit searches all things, even the depths of God. For who among men knows the thoughts of a man except the spirit of the man, which is in him? Even so the thoughts of God no one knows except the Spirit of God." 1 Corinthians 2:10-11

"That the God of our Lord Jesus Christ, the Father of glory, may give to you the spirit of wisdom and revelation in the knowledge of Him," Ephesians 1:17

God asked Solomon to request anything of Him and He would grant it to him. The one thing he requested was wisdom to rule his kingdom and God provided for Solomon. Holy Spirit was with Solomon, just as He was with his father David. He revealed to these men, and many others throughout history, the instruction, direction, strategies and wisdom of God.

Many times, since I received Holy Spirit into my life, He has revealed so much to me. From personal, business to ministry assignments, Holy Spirit has been a crucial aspect of walking out God's plans and purposes in my life. I seek Him daily for wisdom and revelation. I want to know God's will in every area of my life. I spent too many years assuming I knew what God wanted and what He was saying, only to find myself "circling the wilderness" repenting at every turn, because of disobedience. As I surrendered to the Spirit of God within, the communication has exploded through dreams, visions, the Word of God and yes, through great seasons of intercession. I would not trade this precious time with Holy Spirit for anything else in *this* world.

If you are a born-again Believer and have been struggling in your prayer life, as well as in your walk with the Lord, I urge you if you have not already, to acknowledge and receive the Spirit within.

Activate His assignment in your life and allow Him to be the *Intercessor* and *Revealer* God has purposed for Him. I promise you, your life will never be the same again. Your relationship with God will grow deeper and you will find yourself partnering with the God of Creation for the redemption of mankind. We should all, that have called upon the name of Jesus, seek this special privilege of partnering in intercession with the Spirit of God and receiving the wisdom, knowledge, understanding and yes, revelation of God through the *Revealer...Holy Spirit.*

Reinhard Bonnke

"We may sing 'welcome, welcome, Holy Spirit', but He does not come because of our welcome. He is no guest, no stranger invited in for an hour or two. He is the Lord from heaven and He invites us into His presence."

"You must desire the fire, and claim your flame!"
~Reinhard Bonnke

173

Chapter 12
The Indwelling/Infilling of Holy Spirit

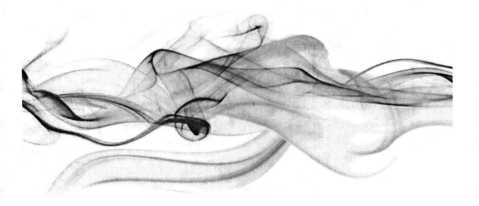

"But if the Spirit of Him who raised Jesus from the dead dwells in you, He who raised Christ Jesus from the dead will also give life to your mortal bodies through His Spirit who indwells you." Romans 8:11

The indwelling power of Holy Spirit within the life of a Believer is probably the single most extraordinary thing to experience, other than salvation, on this earth. He is the closest thing to Heaven on earth that we have; the closest we have to the touch of eternity. To have the Holy One abiding within these mortal bodies is nothing short of miraculous. At the moment of salvation, He takes up permanent habitation in the life of the Believer.

The word *indwelling* means to be permanently present in (someone's soul or mind); possess spiritually. The Hebrew meaning of indwelling in the ancient Talmud is translated *Shekinah*, a Chaldee word, which means presence of God on earth or a symbol or manifestation of His presence. It also means the dwelling or settling divine presence of God, especially in the Temple in Jerusalem. The glory of God, His presence, came upon, or rested upon several different people in the Old Testament, as well as was revealed in several instances of importance in the Word of God. Let's look at a few. One instance, very well known to many, is when the children of Israel were led into the wilderness from Egypt.

"And the LORD went before them by day in a pillar of cloud to lead the way, and by night in a pillar of fire to give them light, so as to go by day and night. He did not take away the pillar of cloud by day or the pillar of fire by night from before the people." Exodus 13:21-22

This is such a powerful display of God's love for His people. He was walking with them every step of the way. Truly a glimpse of God's promise that He will never leave us nor forsake us. His Word is timeless! Another instance of God's presence, or glory, was upon Mount Sinai with their leader Moses was given the Ten Commandments:

"Then it came to pass on the third day, in the morning, that there were thunderings and lightnings, and a thick cloud on the mountain; and the sound of the trumpet was very loud, so that all the people who were in the camp trembled. And Moses brought the people out of the camp to meet with God, and they stood at the foot of the mountain. Now Mount Sinai was completely in smoke, because the LORD descended upon it in fire. Its smoke ascended like the smoke of a furnace, and the whole mountain quaked greatly. And when the blast of the trumpet sounded long and became louder and louder, Moses spoke, and God answered him by voice. Then the LORD came down upon Mount Sinai, on the top of the mountain. And the LORD called Moses to the top of the mountain, and Moses went up." Exodus 19:16-20

This was the Spirit of the Lord "dwelling" at a specific location for a specific purpose. He came in the form of a cloud, but this time, He was preceded with thunderings, lightnings, as well as the sound of a trumpet, and was visible and audible not only to Moses, but to the children of Israel at the base of the mountain in the camp.

The last instance we will discuss is the manifest presence of God's glory in the Tabernacle. This was considered the first place "built" for worship and sacrifice, as well as to house the glory of the Lord; a place where Israel began to know that God Himself was leading them strategically. It was a literal tent.

"Then the cloud covered the tabernacle of meeting, and the glory of the LORD filled the tabernacle. And Moses was not able to enter the tabernacle of meeting, because the cloud rested above it, and the glory of the LORD filled the tabernacle. Whenever the cloud was taken up from above the tabernacle, the children of Israel would go onward in all their journeys. But if the cloud was not taken up, then they did not journey till the day that it was taken up. For the cloud of the LORD was above the tabernacle by day, and fire was over it by night, in the sight of all the house of Israel, throughout all their journeys." Exodus 40:34-38

Before Jesus Christ, Holy Spirit would only appear, or manifest Himself, for specific purposes in people's lives to empower them to carry out His will or in major situations that God needed His people to hear His voice. They did not have the Spirit of God dwelling within them, as we do today, but He was leading His people and dwelling with His precious Israel.

From the wilderness, the Ark of the Covenant (the presence, or glory of God) was built as directed by God, and placed in the Tabernacle, or the Tent of Meetings. That glory was symbolized by the arc which dwelt inside the Most Holy. It was a box about four feet long, gold covered within and without surmounted by two solid gold figures of winged cherubim, this was the place where the High Priest met with God once a year to offer sacrifices for the sins of the children of Israel. The children of Israel carried it on their journey through the wilderness toward the Promised Land. After being captured by the Philistines and later recovered after about eighty years, the Ark of the Covenant in physical form was placed in the Tabernacle in Jerusalem. After five hundred years of the glory of God leading His people, King Solomon ushered in a new era of the erecting of a physical house, or temple, to worship and offer sacrifices to the Lord God, The Temple Mount of Jerusalem. This is the last known Biblical sighting of the Ark of the Covenant (His Presence), according to the Book of Isaiah:

"And Hezekiah received the letter from the hand of the messengers, and read it; and Hezekiah went up to the house of the LORD, and spread it before the LORD. Then Hezekiah prayed to the LORD, saying: "O LORD of hosts, God of Israel, the One who dwells between the cherubim, You are God, You alone, of all the kingdoms of the earth. You have made heaven and earth." Isaiah 37:14-16

My heart grieves as I ponder a people without the presence, or glory of God, once knowing that He led them by fire at night and by a cloud by day. We know that the symbols in the Old Testament were just a foreshadow of what was to come. Because of the sacrifice of the Lamb of God, Jesus Christ, there was no more need of yearly blood sacrifices for the atonement of sins, there was no longer a need for a high priest to go into the presence of God for man, because the Great High Priest entered the Holy of Holies, once and for all, and we now have unlimited access to God through His presence, the indwelling power of Holy Spirit.

The *indwelling* of Holy Spirit is a one time event. Once He is received, He sets up residence within the life of the Believer. The indwelling of Holy Spirit and the baptism of Holy Spirit are one in the same. It is a "sealing" from God of those that are His; those that have chosen to believe that His Son Jesus Christ is, indeed, the Son of God and that He died and rose from the dead for our sins. The *indwelling* power of God within frees us from the flesh and gives us life through His Spirit, *Holy Spirit.*

"So then, those who are in the flesh cannot please God. But you are not in the flesh but in the Spirit, if indeed the Spirit of God dwells in you. Now if anyone does not have the Spirit of Christ, he is not His. And if Christ is in you, the body is dead because of sin, but the Spirit is life because of righteousness. But if the Spirit of Him who raised Jesus from the dead dwells in you, He who raised Christ from the dead will also give life to your mortal bodies through His Spirit who dwells in you." Romans 8:8-11

There is a separate instance that takes places in the life of a Believer that has the indwelling power of Holy Spirit. It is called "filling," or "infilling". This can take place many times throughout a Believer's life. While the *indwelling* of the Spirit happens at conversion, the *infilling* of the Spirit happens continually. Infilling deals with empowering the Believer to live a godly life in service to their family, community of Believers and the world, as well as for service.

"And do not be drunk with wine, in which is dissipation; but be *filled* with the Spirit, speaking to one another in psalms and hymns and spiritual songs, singing and making melody in your heart to the Lord, giving thanks always for all things to God the Father in the name of our Lord Jesus Christ, submitting to one another in the fear of God." Ephesians 5:18-21, emphasis

We can have Holy Spirit dwelling within us, yet never activate His power within our lives. Have you ever met someone that says they are a born-again Believer in Christ Jesus, but is the meanest person you have ever met? This is because they are void of the power of Holy Spirit, filled with Him, that is able to transform our lives and cause us to bear the fruit of the Spirit. We should ask God daily to fill us with His Spirit, so we are able to live and love like our Lord. We are empowered to live Christ like lives through the *infilling* of Holy Spirit.

Another reason for *infilling* is for a specific task or assignment. There is a supernatural level of power needed to carry it out for the Lord. One of the greatest instances of *infilling* for service in the Word of God is that of David. Samuel the Prophet came to Jesse to find out which one of his sons the Lord had chosen.

"And the LORD said, "Arise, anoint him; for this is the one!" Then Samuel took the horn of oil and anointed him in the midst of his brothers; and the Spirit of the LORD came upon David from that day forward." 1 Samuel 16:12-13a

David's assignment is one of the greatest in the Word of God. He was prepared as a young boy in the sheep pastures to become the King of Israel that would ultimately usher from his lineage our Lord and Savior, Jesus Christ. David is credited with some of the greatest feats in the Word of God. God will empower mere mortal bodies with the supernatural *indwelling* power of Holy Spirit to carry out His heavenly plans in the earth realm.

Our brothers and sisters before us, the disciples that walked with our Lord, had the Word (Jesus) with them, walking, talking and doing the work of the Kingdom alongside of Him. The supernatural power of God touched them, ate with them, fellowshipped with them and lived with them. It was not until He left the earth that there was a need to have the *indwelling* and *infilling* power of God with them everywhere they went and at all times. Many were empowered each time they were near Him, but He was the only one at that time to have Holy Spirit dwelling on the inside of Him. As John the Baptist stated:

"I indeed baptize you with water unto repentance, but He who is coming after me is mightier than I, whose sandals I am not worthy to carry. He will baptize you with the Holy Spirit and fire." Matthew 3:11

Fire was used symbolically in Israel's worship to represent God's constant presence with Israel. God's presence as fire represented both judgment and purification. To be in God's presence is to be in the presence of absolute holiness where no sin or unrighteousness can stand. To be in the presence of God is to have the overwhelming sense of one's uncleanness and the overwhelming desire to be clean. God is able to judge and destroy the sin and purify the repentant sinner. Two words that deal with fire in this context are *Purify* and *Purge*.

Purify means to make pure; to clear from material defilement or imperfection; to free from guilt or moral or ceremonial blemish; to free from undesirable elements. The Hebrew word is *zaqaq* meaning to refine, purify, or purge. *Purge* means to clear of guilt or to free from moral or ceremonial defilement. The Hebrew word is *barar* meaning to purify, select, cleanse, or polish. The *indwelling* work of Holy Spirit within the life of a Believer purifies and purges us of our sinful nature causing us to be the righteousness of God in Christ Jesus. The continual *infilling* is the progressive work of Holy Spirit that empowers us, encourages us and equips us to continue pulling from the supernatural power of God.

After His Resurrection, Jesus commissioned His disciples to be His witnesses throughout the earth. He was providing them with the *indwelling* power of Holy Spirit:

"So Jesus said to them again, "Peace to you! As the Father has sent Me, I also send you." And when He had said this, He breathed on them, and said to them, "Receive the Holy Spirit." John 20:211-22

We then see Him, before His ascension, explain to the disciples to wait for the Promise of Holy Spirit. Wait? Didn't they just receive Holy Spirit? Why then would He tell them to wait for Him again? This is a separate gift from *indwelling*; this is now the *infilling*.

"But you shall receive power when the Holy Spirit has come upon you; and you shall be witnesses to Me in Jerusalem, and in all Judea and Samaria, and to the end of the earth." Acts 1:8

The key word in this scripture is "come upon you". The *indwelling* deals with the permanent inward residence of Holy Spirit within our lives. The *infilling* reveals the supernatural power of God through Holy Spirit "coming upon us" for a specific assignment, or purpose. One such instance is on what is considered "The Day of Pentecost".

"When the Day of Pentecost had fully come, they were all with one accord in one place. And suddenly there came a sound from heaven, as of a rushing mighty wind, and it filled the whole house where they were sitting. Then there appeared to them divided tongues, as of fire, and one sat upon each of them. And they were all filled with the Holy Spirit and began to speak with other tongues, as the Spirit gave them utterance." Acts 2:1-4

One manifestation of the *infilling* of Holy Spirit is that of speaking in other tongues, or commonly known as our "heavenly language". This is one of the greatest debates amongst born-again Believers throughout Christendom. Some don't believe in it, some believe, yet don't operate in it, while others completely believe in it, yet operate completely out of order with the manifestation. I am not here to debate, but to provide sound biblical directive concerning this most precious gift from the Father. Now, we can either believe all of scripture, the full counsel of God, or as I've stated many times throughout this book, none at all. I think the best way to approach this is to simply believe what the Word says...period. If Jesus commanded the disciples to wait for the Promise of Holy Spirit, then it must have been extremely important to do so, and to understand that this would be a separate manifestation than the *indwelling*. It did not say just one, or a few of them, was filled; it says *all*. According to the Word of God, there were about one hundred and twenty people in this house.

From the beginning of Creation, man spoke one language. After the fall of Adam, they continued to speak in uniformity until around Genesis chapter eleven when a rebellion arose and the people joined together to build what was called the "Tower of Babel," designed to reach all the way to heaven to prove they would rule themselves, not God. They were conspiring to replace God in their hearts and the hearts of all around the world. The word *babel* means a confusion of sounds or voices; a scene of noise or confusion. The Hebrew translation means to confuse or confound the language. It was at this place, in the land of Shinar, where God confused the languages of the people and scattered them all throughout the earth. Yes, the earth was, at one point, of one language. It his highly regarded that on the Day of Pentecost, the *infilling* of Holy Spirit that was subsequently proceeded by "other tongues" was a reversal of God's curse of divided languages.

After the scattering of Babel, people would travel back to Jerusalem each year for the feasts and celebrations. On this particular day, about fifty days after Jesus' death and about ten days after ascension, the disciples were all held up in prayer and worship awaiting the Promise of God. Jews from all over the known world at that time were coming to celebrate the firstfruits of the wheat harvest, interestingly enough, exactly fifty days after the Passover feast. As they were celebrating, they heard something that completely baffled each of them:

> "And there were dwelling in Jerusalem Jews, devout men, from every nation under heaven. And when this sound occurred, the multitude came together, and were confused, because everyone heard them speak in his own language. Then they were all amazed and marveled, saying to one another, "Look, are not all these who speak Galileans? And how is it that we hear, each in our own language in which we were born? Parthians and Medes and Elamites, those dwelling in Mesopotamia, Judea and Cappadocia, Pontus and Asia, Phrygia and Pamphylia, Egypt and the parts of Libya adjoining Cyrene, visitors from Rome, both Jews and proselytes, Cretans and Arabs—we hear them speaking in our own tongues the wonderful works of God." So they were all amazed and perplexed, saying to one another, "Whatever could this mean?" Acts 2:5-12

So we see here that God used this *kairos* moment in time not only to release His Spirit upon all the disciples for the work of the Kingdom, but also to restore and reconcile many that were scattered throughout the earth with this miraculous manifestation. Not all believed, but some could not deny it if they chose. These unlearned Galileans were speaking languages they could have never learned. This had to be the hand of God Almighty! The tongues ceased when Peter got up to preach. Interestingly enough, his choice text for this gathering was out of the Book of Joel.

> "But this is what was spoken by the prophet Joel: 'And it shall come to pass in the last days, says God, That I will pour out of My Spirit on all flesh; your sons and your daughters shall prophesy, your young men shall see visions, your old men shall dream dreams. And on My menservants and on My maidser-

vants I will pour out My Spirit in those days; and they shall prophesy. I will show wonders in heaven above and signs in the earth beneath: Blood and fire and vapor of smoke. The sun shall be turned into darkness, and the moon into blood, before the coming of the great and awesome day of the LORD. And it shall come to pass that whoever calls on the name of the LORD shall be saved.'" Joel 2:28-32

Peter was confirming that what these devout Jews were witnessing was not a "drunken stupor" from the disciples, but a prophetic fulfillment, or at a least a partial fulfillment, of the prophet Joel. These Jews were devout, meaning they were students of scripture, so they could not deny its authenticity, even though some chose to do so. The promise of Joel is that God will pour out His Spirit upon *all* flesh. It was seen on the day of Pentecost, and we are seeing it happen at miraculous rates even today. God's Word is Truth and not one Word of it has yet to fall to the ground.

This *formula*, if you will, or *blueprint*, provided by Jesus Christ, did so much more than empower the disciples and encourage the listeners. The effects of this *infilling* of Holy Spirit, with the following dispersement of heavenly tongues, caused Jerusalem to be turned upside down for the Kingdom of God! What took place following this is nothing short of the hand of God!

"And with many other words he testified and exhorted them, saying, "Be saved from this perverse generation." Then those who gladly received his word were baptized; and that day about three thousand souls were added to them. And they continued steadfastly in the apostles' doctrine and fellowship, in the breaking of bread, and in prayers. Then fear came upon every soul, and many wonders and signs were done through the apostles. Now all who believed were together, and had all things in common, and sold their possessions and goods, and divided them among all, as anyone had need. So continuing daily with one accord in the temple, and breaking bread from house to house, they ate their food with gladness and simplicity of heart, praising God and having favor with all the people. And the Lord added to the church daily those who were being saved." Acts 2:40-47

You cannot convince me that the *infilling* of Holy Spirit and the manifestation of speaking in tongues, our heavenly language, is not directly tied to God's perfect will and is a part of His redemptive work in mankind. The evidence is not the tongues; the evidence is the fruit! An entire community was forever changed, and those that traveled back to their homes across the world, carried these miraculous tools back with them, building God's Kingdom in the earth. What is produced out of faith in God's living, breathing Word? Line upon line…precept upon precept…the *full counsel* of God's Word.

There is another instance in Acts where Peter was preaching to a group of Gentiles of the household of Cornelius, as well as many of his friends. As he was preaching, something miraculous happened:

"While Peter was still speaking these words, the Holy Spirit fell upon all those who heard the word. And those of the circumcision who believed were astonished, as many as came with Peter, because the gift of the Holy Spirit had been poured out on the Gentiles also. For they heard them speak with tongues and magnify God." Acts 10:44-46

Before now, the Jews were the only ones receiving the baptism of fire, or Holy Spirit. Peter was specifically sent by God to the Gentiles to witness Jesus Christ to reveal that it was His desire that all men be saved and those that believed, spoke with tongues and magnified God, *all* of them. There were others that traveled with Peter, it says those of the "circumcision," also known as Jews, were astonished. It says here it was the "gift of Holy Spirit". Again, a separate manifestation from the *indwelling*.

The Indwelling/Infilling of Holy Spirit

In another location, Paul was at Ephesus and he found some of the disciples in the upper hill country. He questioned them if they had received Holy Spirit when they believed. They explained they had no such knowledge of Holy Spirit, so Paul asked them into what baptism did they receive. They told him, "Into John's baptism." This is Paul's response:

> "Then Paul said, "John indeed baptized with a baptism of repentance, saying to the people that they should believe on Him who would come after him, that is, on Christ Jesus." When they heard this, they were baptized in the name of the Lord Jesus. And when Paul had laid hands on them, the Holy Spirit came upon them, and they spoke with tongues and prophesied. Now the men were about twelve in all." Acts 19:4-6

Once again, we see that Holy Spirit "came upon them" and they, twelve in all, spoke with tongues, as well as prophesied. So, receiving the *infilling* of Holy Spirit with the evidence of speaking in tongues is not a "random" occurrence, at least not in Biblical reference. These are the very words of our Lord, Jesus Christ:

> "And He said to them, "Go into all the world and preach the gospel to every creature. He who believes and is baptized will be saved; but he who does not believe will be condemned. And these signs will follow those who believe: In My name they will cast out demons; they will *speak with new tongues*; they will take up serpents; and if they drink anything deadly, it will by no means hurt them; they will lay hands on the sick, and they will recover." Mark 16:15-18, emphasis

I firmly believe the key aspect in all of these occurrences is the preceding statement, "those that believe". Do I believe it is available to all? Yes. Do I believe all will receive? No. It is that simple. Does that make a person not a born-again Believer? Absolutely not, but I do believe those that have chosen to believe and receive the *infilling* of Holy Spirit with the evidence of speaking in other tongues will do supernatural exploits for Jesus Christ in the earth realm. It is just as our Lord stated, "In My name they will cast out demons; they will speak with new tongues; they will take up serpents; and if they drink anything deadly, it will by no means hurt them; they will lay hands on the sick, and they will recover." These are supernatural manifestations that only those that believe in them will do them. This does not make them better than someone that does not; it just means that someone is crazy enough to believe God! And I am one of them! I choose to believe the Word of God, the full counsel...*all of it!*

Now I have been privy to the notion of speaking in tongues since I was twelve years old. I was not raised in a church that preached about it or operated in it; in fact, it was a very reserved United Methodist church that you could hear a pin drop in, because of the solemn tone in which we worshipped. It was not until my father was diagnosed with cancer that he took us to another church, that being Pentecostal. The music was very "high spirited" and they had an entire band with every instrument you could think of, unlike our church organ that had the ability to put you to sleep right in the middle of service. It was kind of fun, surely not something I was used to, but I could tell people were happy. I joined in the song and dance and it felt good, until the music stopped and now it sounded like people were speaking in another language? I became confused. I had never heard this before and I could not understand what they were saying. I was eventually saved at this church, but I did not receive Holy Spirit, or at least I did not know, at the time, that Holy Spirit was within me, at this point of salvation. I just knew I wasn't speaking in this crazy language.

Years passed, and I returned to the Lord after a while of being away from the church and from God. I rededicated my life to the Lord and about three years later, I desired more from God. There was something missing in my walk with Him. I felt stagnant and stale. I knew there had to be more to God than what I was experiencing. I finally chose to study the Word of God in the area of

Holy Spirit and speaking in tongues. I found that the same way I could believe that Jesus died for me and rose again for my sins; I could believe He sent Holy Spirit to comfort me, lead me, instruct me and equip me to do what God had called me to do for His Kingdom. Going back to the Pentecostal church I attended at twelve, people who chose to go to the altar to receive this gift were getting hit in the stomach, slapped with cloths and "blown" on by the pastor; just too weird for me. This church I was now at was just a non-denominational church, but they did believe in speaking in tongues. I went up to receive, both my husband and I, and they prayed over him and he fell to the floor and eventually, began to speak in tongues. That did not happen with me. I believed whole-heartedly and desired a closer walk with God, but the manifestation did not happen for me at that time. I have to say I was pretty devastated. I began to question if I really believed. My husband was shortly called overseas to Germany with the military. He went ahead of us in January and I was to meet him in March.

I was in my living room one night after putting my children to bed. I got my Bible and notebook and sat down to study the Word. I turned on some Worship music and turned in my notebook to a sermon on Holy Spirit. I began going over the notes I had taken and one scripture that just popped off of the page to me was in Jude:

"But you, beloved, building yourselves up on your most holy faith, praying in the Holy Spirit," Jude 20

Did I have faith? I know I believed, but did I have faith? Did I doubt somewhere? Were my motives wrong? The next scripture that jumped off of the page was:

"Now faith is the substance of things hoped for, the evidence of things not seen." Hebrews 11:1

Was I too busy looking at how I "thought" it was done? How I "thought" it should look? I always saw people fall out on the floor and I didn't want to fall. I didn't want someone to hit me in my stomach, hit me with a cloth or "blow" on me. As a light bulb went on inside of me from these scriptures, I knew it wasn't this "spooky" or "magical" thing I expected, or even a show of foolish display that would hurt me. As I sat on my couch, tears began to roll down my face and I felt an overwhelming presence of love surrounding me. I heard the voice of God say, "Receive Me now." I was startled, because I had never heard His voice before. Crazy enough, my lights flickered, of which I can now sit back and laugh at, but at the time, I was so serious that I wanted this gift from God. I closed my eyes and began to pray. I prayed for about five minutes, thanking God for loving me and literally, out of my belly began to flow tongues, my heavenly language.

"He that believeth on me, as the scripture hath said, out of his belly shall flow rivers of living water." John 7:38, KJV

I did not force it, I did not stop it…it just flowed out me and everything inside of me just let go and I prayed in my heavenly language for almost an hour. I literally fell asleep in the presence of Father God. I woke up on my living room floor and I have never been the same since. Every part of my life began to grow, as a wife, a mother, a friend and a servant of God. My prayer life went to another realm and it was from here that I journeyed to Germany to meet my husband. It was not too long after I received the *infilling* of Holy Spirit that I was prophesied over that God was calling me to intercede for the nations of the world. My dreams also began to open up greatly and with great purpose through intercession. I was now seeing the promise of Jude 20. I was truly being built up on my most holy of faith as I prayed every day in the Spirit.

Speaking in tongues, as it relates to the individual Believer, is absolutely crucial to our faith. It is an enhancer in every sense of the word and opens up our spirit to Holy Spirit's leading and instruction. I have received great instruction and direction out my deepest times of praying in my heavenly language. Now many, as I stated earlier, can and have taken this precious gift and used it erroneously and out of order. We must read the Word of God and heed its truths. Praying in the Spirit, or speaking in tongues, is primarily for the edifying of the individual Believer. It can also be a tool in equipping someone for a very important spiritual assignment. We don't know what we are praying when we pray in the Spirit, but God does, and it is a part of His ultimate will for our lives.

"Likewise the Spirit also helps in our weaknesses. For we do not know what we should pray for as we ought, but the Spirit Himself makes intercession for us with groanings which cannot be uttered. Now He who searches the hearts knows what the mind of the Spirit is, because He makes intercession for the saints according to the will of God." Romans 8:26-27

Holy Spirit is working within us as we pray in the Spirit and relaying the mind and heart of God, His will, in our lives. We are spiritual beings and when we surrender our earthly limitations and trust in the Living God, we release the supernatural power of God to invade every area of our lives for His glory. As we speak in tongues, He makes intercession for us, because He is able to accurately discern not only what is in our hearts, but also what the perfect will is of Father God. What an amazing blessing to have such a gift here in the earth realm. I know many do not believe, but if you can believe that God sent His only Son into the earth realm through the conduit of a woman, not touched by man, but Holy Spirit "came upon her" and she conceived, then how can we not believe that this same Holy Spirit can "come upon us" and empower us to do that which is not earthly possible to do? It is absolutely scriptural and would not be included if it was not crucial to God's plan in our lives.

Let's delve a little further. Praying in the Spirit in corporate settings has an entirely different order to it; the Word of God clearly states that there are guidelines to adhere by, so that there is no confusion to the Believer or unbeliever. I have witnessed many different practices all over the world, and had to unlearn a lot of what I was taught concerning speaking in tongues, as some of it was not scriptural.

"He who speaks in a tongue edifies himself, but he who prophesies edifies the church. I wish you all spoke with tongues, but even more that you prophesied; for he who prophesies is greater than he who speaks with tongues, unless indeed he interprets, that the church may receive edification." 1 Corinthians 14:4-5

If tongues are spoken in a corporate setting, interpretation should follow. I have been in services where the "gift of tongues" was manifested and the prophet of this house interpreted her own tongue. It was the first time I have ever witnessed such a manifestation of the Spirit, but it was such an authentic encounter with the Living God that it was undeniable. The entire church fell on their knees and all you could hear was weeping. God had spoken through this prophet of God through the "gift of tongues," and subsequently, its interpretation. The Body was truly edified through this Word from God and this was absolute Biblical order. The "gift of tongues," or "different tongues," is not the same as speaking in tongues. Let's look at a few scriptures to clarify:

"And there are diversities of activities, but it is the same God who works all in all. But the manifestation of the Spirit is given to each one for the profit of all: for to one is given the word of wisdom through the Spirit, to another the word of knowledge through the same Spirit, to another faith by the same Spirit, to another gifts of healings by the same Spirit, to another the working of miracles, to another prophecy, to another discerning of spirits, to another *different kinds of tongues*, to another the interpretation of tongues. But one and the same Spirit works all these things, distributing to each one individually as He wills." 1 Corinthians 12:6-11

I, too, have received the manifestation of *different tongues* over the years. I used to question it, because it just did not make sense to my natural mind. I was ordained in Germany in prophetic gifting in 2007. I had been speaking in my heavenly language for about seven years now, and interceding greatly. I could sense God taking me deeper, but I was continually fighting Him, because I was truly being taken out of my comfort zone. I was always a timid person. I did not like being around large crowds, let alone speaking in front of anyone. My pastor began to call me out in services to lay hands on people to be healed, as well as to give what the Lord was speaking for the church. I was being "groomed" for the prophetic ministry. I began hearing Holy Spirit in ways I had never before heard Him. We received military orders to leave Germany. Our last church service before we left, Holy Spirit invaded my entire being. We were in prayer during the offering, and all of a sudden, my mouth opened and the Spirit gave me utterance. I had absolutely no control whatsoever over my tongue. I had witnessed our church prophet operate in this gift for several years, and ironically, I was sitting right beside her. I immediately began to weep and then fear came over me. I began rebuking the devil, because I was not the prophet of this house and I felt as if I stepped out of order. Suddenly, I felt a hand grab my hand and she said, "Open your mouth and speak." And I did just that. This was the first time I had spoken in *other tongues* and interpreted by the Spirit of God.

The spiritual gift of interpretation of tongues is found alongside the gift of speaking in tongues. The Greek word for interpretation is *hermeneia* and simply means to interpret, explain, or expound some message that is not able to be understood in a natural way. Thus, this spiritual gift is the supernatural ability to understand and explain messages uttered in an unknown language. This is a revelatory gift, meaning that God "reveals" the meaning of the words or message being spoken and allows the interpreter to communicate its meaning to those who need to hear it. When this happens in the church two things happen: the church is edified and God is glorified. The spiritual gift of interpretation is given by Holy Spirit to certain individuals to reveal messages spoken in an unknown tongue to God for the building up of the church. Like the gift of prophecy, tongues that are interpreted have the effect of encouraging and blessing the church to love and serve God more deeply and effectively.

This gift of *other tongues* and *interpretation* is not given to all Believers, but to some, for the edifying and encouraging of the Body of Christ. But the *infilling* of Holy Spirit is able to produce the evidence of speaking in tongues for those that believe and receive the Promisē left for us by our Lord and Savior, Jesus Christ. If you believe today, you can receive Holy Spirit into your life through the supernatural *infilling* of the power of God, *and* the manifestation of speaking in your heavenly language. The Word of God says to simply ask:

"If you then, being evil, know how to give good gifts to your children, how much more will your heavenly Father give the Holy Spirit to those who ask Him!" Luke 11:13

There are many benefits to the *indwelling* and *infilling* power of Holy Spirit in the lives of born again Believers. The multi-faceted prism of Holy Spirit serves humanity in ways unimaginable, but ultimately, He helps us to bring others into the Kingdom of God.

"And when they had prayed, the place where they had gathered together was shaken, and they were all filled with the Holy Spirit and began to speak the word of God with boldness." Acts 4:31

As Believers, we are all commissioned to spread the Gospel of Jesus Christ in whatever sphere of influence we have been given.

Whether it is our home, our workplace, or just out an about in our everyday lives, we are called to tell others about Jesus. Without the *indwelling* power of Holy Spirit, most of us will never share our faith with others. We are either afraid of what people will say, the fear of rejection, or we feel we are not qualified enough to witness. Sharing Jesus is not just the job of your pastor or spiritual leaders; Jesus has commanded us all to go into the entire world baptizing in the name of the Father, the Son and yes, *Holy Spirit*. He provides us super-natural boldness to turn this world upside down for Jesus!

I will leave you with one of the most powerful scriptures in the Word of God concerning Holy Spirit from the man after God's own heart...David.

"Do not cast me away from Your presence, And do not take Your Holy Spirit from me..." Psalm 51:11

D.L. Moody

"We all need it [the filling of the Holy Spirit] together, and let us not rest day nor night until we possess it; if that is the uppermost thought in our hearts, God will give it to us if we just hunger and thirst for it and say, 'God helping me, I will not rest until endued with power from on high.'"

"There is no better evangelist in the world than the Holy Spirit."
~D.L. Moody

Chapter 13

The Voice
of Holy Spirit

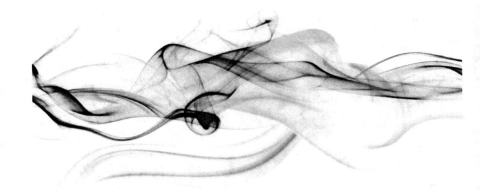

"But when He, the Spirit of truth, comes, He will guide you into all the truth; for He will not speak on His own initiative, but whatever He hears, He will speak; and He will disclose to you what is to come." John 16:13

The Old Testament is full of people that reaped great relationship with Holy Spirit and depended upon His Voice to lead, guide, direct and instruct them in every area of their lives. They received Him as the gift He was, and is, and followed His leading. Though He was not a permanent dwelling place in their lives, they honored and respected His role, and when He revealed Himself to them, they listened and subsequently, obeyed His voice. Sadly, we have Holy Spirit available to us without measure. He dwells within the life of every born-again Believer, yet many of us neglect the gift many of our fathers in the faith desired.

In today's Christian circles, it is either all of Holy Spirit, or absolutely none. Those that are all for Holy Spirit's assignment in the earth realm, at least many of them, are so enthralled by the "supernatural" that they neglect His voice speaking through the Word of God and claim they only hear His voice by Holy Spirit, or some sort of prophetic gift. This is error. As I stated earlier, the Word will never contradict the Spirit, and vice-versa. Just as in the infilling of Holy Spirit as the disciples tarried in the Upper Room, afterward, Peter preached the Word of God that complimented what just took place "in the Spirit". It is neither one nor the other; they must coincide to reveal the full intent of God's voice to His people. Because many reject this, they usually go off into crazy rants of spiritual phenomena that are absolutely contradictory to sound Biblical doctrine. For some, it can lead into great carnality and worldliness, while for others, it leads to open doors of demonic manifestations, new age spiritualism and cult-like meetings. Their desire is not the true, authentic voice of God, but earthly and sensual manifestations or supernatural occurrences that tickle their senses and entertain. Holy Spirit is not a "side show," neither is He some sort of puppet we lead and guide to do what we want Him to do. But we see this far too often in today's church world, and it is devastating to the Body of Christ as a whole, because it runs people away from the true, authentic voice of Holy Spirit.

Those that completely reject Holy Spirit in the beginning and say they only hear from God through the Word are also in error. Just as the scripture states, "The letter kills, but the Spirit gives life." These believers will completely stand upon the "law" of the Word, and neglect the grace that not only came through Jesus, but through the indwelling power of God within us, *Holy Spirit*. He is also known as the Spirit of Grace. These two extremes serve to further eradicate the assignment of Holy Spirit within the church today. But glory to God, He has all things in the palm of His hands, and He has faithful followers all around the world that are being led by His voice, the voice of Holy Spirit. The Hebrew word "to hear" is *shama*. It also means attentively, call or gather together, carefully, certainly, consent, or consider. The Greek word is *akouó* meaning to hear, listen, give audience, come to the ears, or be reported.

I get so many people that ask me how I hear from God the way I do; and how they can learn to hear from Him, as well. The most important way to know you are hearing from God is to line it up with Scripture. A lifestyle of reading the Word of God and meditating upon it day and night will provide us great stability when it comes to discerning what is God and what is not. The Word of God was written by holy men of God that were "inspired" by Holy Spirit. He will speak through the Word of God to you the same way He spoke to the prophets, disciples and fathers of our faith to write it. Don't look at the Word of God as a storybook filled with great parables, wisdom and life lessons; it is literally the living, breathing, Spirit-filled voice of God to His people. When we settle this is our hearts, our minds and our spirits, we will never read the Word of God the same again. It will become life to our dead bones; sustenance for our starving souls. We will cling to every word and it will begin to take form within our lives. We will no longer just know the Word; we will *be* the Word!

"And the Word became flesh and dwelt among us, and we beheld His glory, the glory as of the only begotten of the Father, full of grace and truth." John 1:14

Just as Jesus was the embodiment of Scripture, we, too, are to become the living, breathing prophetic manifestation of the written Word of God. He desires for us to be so transformed by His Word that the world will see Him through us. If the world cannot look at us and "read" us as if it is the Word, then we have not allowed this very Word to transform our lives. We are called to be living epistles, read by men. (2 Corinthians 3:2) It is no longer about knowing the scripture to have it memorized; we are commanded to embody it. This is another revelation altogether. It will separate those that want a church experience from those who hunger and thirst for the fullness of God in their lives.

The next important tool is that of Worship. Our Father is to be glorified. We were created to Worship Him. It is in the secret place of Worship where we begin to know who He truly is; His sovereignty and His majesty. Many equate Worship to two praise songs and a slow song at church and that is the extent of their worship to God. Worship is not carnal, or worldly. It is not something to be taken so lightly or frivolously. God is not a man; worshipping Him is something altogether magnificent and awe inspiring. The Word of God tells us to worship Him in Spirit and in Truth.

"But the hour is coming, and now is, when the true worshipers will worship the Father in spirit and truth; for the Father is seeking such to worship Him. God is Spirit, and those who worship Him must worship in spirit and truth." John 4:23-24

He implies through the Word that there are authentic worshippers; true worshippers; meaning, there are also those that are do not possess authenticity in Worship. One of the most notable Worship leaders of this generation is Darlene Zschech. Her absolute love for God is evident and she is truly that "living epistle read my men". Her worship to God is not an outward display of musical genius, or an attempt to lure you into an experience. Her horizontal relationship with Father God in Worship allows other Believers to vertically witness, or experience, an authentic heart of Worship, leading them to a personal relationship with Him, as well. Here is a quote for Worship Leader magazine[xi]

"I can know a lot about music, a lot about worship, yet still not really know God for myself. Many of us have become so busy that we miss the great blessing of true communion with our Lord and in doing so we can lose the ability to recognize his voice as He speaks to us." ~Darlene Zschech

What a powerful truth! Distraction is one of the greatest enemies of hearing the voice of God. It is very important to remain still and silent, at times, in Worship to hear our Father's voice. All too often, we are pulled to have an "experience," whether it is clapping, jumping, dancing or shouting, which are not bad things at all, but we do these outward things in vain if we cannot hear the voice of God Almighty. We merely get excited about the music and the lyrics, yet miss the adorning love of our King. I have been in many different kinds of Worship services all over the world. I have witnessed many entertainment driven churches with thousands of attendees on their feet applauding the singers and not worshipping the Father. They are void of the Spirit and leave you feeling as if you just left a secular concert. It is a very devastating reality to see man lifted and not the Father. Yet, I have been privileged by God to witness the beauty of authentic worship to the Lord. A room with ten, twenty or fifty at the most, surrendered and submitted to Holy Spirit within and sold out to the Lord. The wind of the Spirit sweeping through at the sound of God's people worshipping yes, *in Spirit and in Truth*.....absolutely priceless! This is the kind of atmosphere where the voice of God invades the earth realm through the conduit of *Holy Spirit*.

I was also privileged to lead prophetic dance ministries in several of the churches I attended over our time in the United States military. This was my outlet of Worship to the Lord; this is how I expressed my love and adoration for Father God, and He opened up the door for me to share my love for Him with other women, as well as children. I took this assignment very seriously. It was not a game, it was not "fun time," it was a time of imparting the love of Worship into others that had barely scratched the surface of intimacy with their Lord. I remember in each church opening with silent Worship for almost an hour, and then prayer. I taught reverence to the presence of God and not to cheapen the time by playing around and neglecting to hear the voice of God. I knew some came because they just wanted to dance; they did not know the importance of Worship. Some wanted to perform, others desired to minister. Authentic Worship opens the door for Holy Spirit to speak.

Finally, we need to exercise our hearing from God in prayer. I know all of this sounds absolutely elementary, but I am here to tell you if we do not get back to the foundations of our faith, the simplicity of the Gospel, then we are going to miss Him altogether. It is upon these foundational truths that we stand firm and planted against the turbulent and chaotic times we are living in. Prayer is not just simply you talking to God and laying out a laundry list of things you desire from Him; authentic prayer is developing an intimate relationship with God where there is not merely monolithic monologue, but Spirit-infused, life-giving dialogue. The word *monologue* means a prolonged talk or discourse by a single speaker, especially one dominating or monopolizing a conversation. The word *dialogue* is polar opposite. It is defined as conversation between two or more persons; an exchange of ideas or opinions on a particular issue, especially a political or religious issue, with a view to reaching an amicable agreement or settlement.

How many Believers are in a one-way relationship with God? They talk to Him, or at Him, yet never hear His voice. God's desire is not only intimate fellowship with His Creation, but He also desires to partner with us to carry out His will in the earth realm. How can He accomplish this when we never learn to hear His voice? Many Believers would rather their pastors or spiritual leaders be the voice of God in their lives. This is very dangerous, because though they may be called to be a shepherd to God's people, they are *not* His voice in their lives. This is how many people fall away from God, because their pastors or spiritual leaders reveal their "humanness" and it will most certainly contradict the voice of God. You can love your pastors or spiritual leaders and pray for them, as they preach the Gospel, but if what they preach goes against the Word of God, you better run as fast as you can out of that church and ask the Lord to lead you to a Word preaching, Holy Spirit filled house of God. Let's listen to the Words of Jesus:

"Jesus answered them, "I told you, and you do not believe. The works that I do in My Father's name, they bear witness of Me. But you do not believe, because you are not of My sheep, as I said to you. My sheep hear My voice, and I know them, and they follow Me. And I give them eternal life, and they shall never perish; neither shall anyone snatch them out of My hand. My Father, who has given them to Me, is greater than all; and no one is able to snatch them out of My Father's hand. I and My Father are one." John 10:25-30

Jesus declares that His sheep *hear His voice* and follow Him. There are many pastors in the church today that are not preaching the Word of God, but many other strange doctrines. When true sheep recognize it and speak upon it, they are called rebels and scolded, yet they know the voice of the Father, because they are *His sheep*, not yours. They have every right to walk out and never come back; because they are not obligated to stay anywhere that false doctrine is being presented. Again, if you are not intimate with the Word of God, you will not know the authentic from the counterfeit. You will accept it, because it sounds good. Be aware, be alert and cover yourself in discernment.

"But the Spirit explicitly says that in later times some will fall away from the faith, paying attention to deceitful spirits and doctrines of demons," 1 Timothy 4:1

The surest way to guard ourselves against such deceit is to stay close to Father God in the Word, Worship and Prayer. Holy Spirit will lead us every step of the way and as we daily open our eyes, ask Him to continually fill us with His precious Spirit. His voice is our guide and another's we will not follow. Be led by Him today!

7 Avenues to Hear the Voice of God in our Lives

❖ The Word
"All Scripture is given by inspiration of God, and is profitable for doctrine, for reproof, for correction, for instruction in righteousness, that the man of God may be complete, thoroughly equipped for every good work." 2 Timothy 3:16-17

I have heard the voice of God many times through the Word, but one instance, in particular, was like a lightning bolt that shot right through me. I sat in church on a Wednesday night for Bible Study. The Worship, as always, was absolutely breathtaking and pure. We are always ushered into the Word of God in His presence, truly the beauty of His holiness. As we sat down to receive the Word, there was such peace in the atmosphere. One of our pastors opened up in 1 Timothy. As He prayed and then proceeded to voice the words of life from the pages of this book of instruction, I heard Holy Spirit say, "Go back!" I knew immediately what He was saying to me and where I was supposed to go back to. I began to weep uncontrollably, as it was not something I wanted to do. I had no instructions on when, for how long, or what I was even supposed to do when I got there, but one thing I did know…it was *HIS VOICE!*

❖ Worship
"O God, You are my God; early will I seek You; My soul thirsts for You; My flesh longs for You in a dry and thirsty land where there is no water. So I have looked for You in the sanctuary, to see Your power and Your glory." Psalms 63:1-2

David worshipped God more than anyone we know of in the Word of God. The entire Book of Psalms is penned by this worshipper, the man after God's own heart. *Psalm* means a sacred song or hymn. There is nothing wrong with corporate Worship, but our lives should display a continual worship of Father God in our everyday coming and going. Our corporate Worship should be

204

an extension of our private Worship. I love to Worship. I can sit for hours in the presence of God in complete adoration. It is a place of solace and comfort for me. Even in the writing of this book, when I felt the blockages and could not write, I would put on Worship and lay on my face before God, and then I would hear the voice of God, Holy Spirit, speak to me and I would get up and just flow in the Spirit, as He led my hands. He speaks, as we Worship Him.

"But the hour is coming, and now is, when the true worshipers will worship the Father in spirit and truth; for the Father is seeking such to worship Him."

❖ Prayer
"Incline your ear, and come to Me. Hear, and your soul shall live; and I will make an everlasting covenant with you—the sure mercies of David." Isaiah 55:3

To be privileged to speak with the God of Heaven...unfathomable! Yet, how many born-again Believers rarely spend time in His presence? We want so badly for Him to give us answers, but how is that possible when we can't even sit in His presence for more than five minutes in prayer? As I stated previously, prayer is monologue and dialogue, giving and receiving. It is relationship. Prayer has always been a huge part of my life. Learning how to move from requests to instructions is a sign of spiritual maturity. Again, I have heard much in prayer over the years, but one situation I hold dear to my heart. I heard from God that He wanted me to lay hands on someone to be healed. This was the first time I heard Him say He would use me in the healing of process of someone. I went to Bible Study that night, and our pastor's wife, who is an amazing woman of prayer, opened up the service in prayer and worship and then proceeded to speak out that God was going to use someone to lay hands to heal someone before the end of that years was out. I knew God was speaking to me. She asked whoever it was to come to the altar and she would anoint them. Several people came forward, which happens in most instances like this, but I know that God, *just that morning*, spoke to me by Holy Spirit, that He was going to do this. She anointed me, and that night, I contacted the precious woman that God laid upon my heart. I explained to her what I heard, and we began fasting and praying, seeking the Father's heart for her healing. About a week before the end of the year, I was fasting and praying, and I heard God say there was a root of unforgiveness that was holding back her healing. I began to strategically intercede for her and contacted her once again and shared what the Lord spoke. Immediately, her spirit was in agreement. She explained there were several people in her life that she needed to offer forgiveness to, as well as healing, deliverance, restoration and reconciliation. She did it; she obeyed the Lord and this began her road to healing.

On New Year's Eve of that year, she met me at my church and we searched all over for an open prayer room or somewhere to pray, but all the doors were locked! She said she would go in the bathroom; she did not care, she was ready to be healed! I anointed her right there in the hallway and we began to stand in agreement for my dear sister's healing. God healed her body that night! Prayer is not just a cute little act we go through, it is direct communication with Father God and He wants to speak to His people. Incline your ear today to hear the voice of God, the voice of Holy Spirit.

❖ Through Other People

"Then Nathan said to David, "You are the man! Thus says the LORD God of Israel: 'I anointed you king over Israel, and I delivered you from the hand of Saul. I gave you your master's house and your master's wives into your keeping, and gave you the house of Israel and Judah. And if that had been too little, I also would have given you much more! Why have you despised the commandment of the LORD, to do evil in His sight?"
2 Samuel 12:7-9

God used Nathan the prophet to speak a Word from Him to David. It wasn't a very *good* Word, but it was the truth; it was necessary to get David where God needed him. He may send someone into our lives to correct us, instruct us, or even bless us, but we must be willing to receive the Word of the Lord from them, so there will be no room for blockage in hearing from God.

❖ Dreams and Visions

"In the first year of Belshazzar king of Babylon, Daniel had a dream and visions of his head while on his bed. Then he wrote down the dream, telling the main facts." Daniel 7:1

I have had prophetic dreams since I was a little girl. I did not know then how prophetic they were, but as I grew in spiritual maturity, and began to see more clearly in dreams and visions, I knew God was speaking to me through them. As I interceded more and more, the more God would open up His heart and mind to me in dreams and visions. I have had more dreams than visions, but one of the dreams had a vision "within it". I was pregnant with my second child. We wanted to know the sex of the baby, so we had an ultrasound scheduled for the same day as my baby shower. The night before, I was very tired, so I went to bed early. As I began to doze off, I was standing in my kitchen making my daughter lunch. I immediately saw a tremendous beam of light enter through my kitchen window; it was totally blinding. I then began to hear children laughing outside of the window. The blinding light faded, and now I was in a vision. I looked out the window and I saw children running and playing everywhere. There were no adults, except for one man in a long red robe standing in the middle of them. I walked to my front door and opened it. As I saw the man, I began to "levitate" towards him; for those that don't know what that is, I was floating in the air towards him. As I approached him, I fell to my face and began to Worship. He lifted up my chin, and I looked up to Him. That blinding light was all around His head, so I could not see His face, but the presence I felt was absolutely overwhelming! I was weeping deeply. He said these words to me,

"Daughter, because you have been faithful, I have blessed you and your husband with a son. You will call him Elijah." The dream ended right there.

Needless to say, I cancelled the ultrasound the next day and began claiming my son, by name, and thanking God for visiting me and speaking to me through His voice...the voice of Holy Spirit.

❖ **Through Life Situations and Circumstances**
"A man's heart plans his way, But the LORD directs his steps." Proverbs 16:9

Many times, we expect to hear an "audible" voice clearly and precisely telling us which direction in which to go. And if we don't hear that, then we are quick to say, "This is not God!" Well, this is so very far from the truth. God can, and absolutely does, speak to His children through life situations and circumstances. It is in these times where we are challenged to trust what we are seeing take place, step by step, instead of hearing that audible voice. I have shared this story many times, but it fits this situation perfectly. I won't go into detail while we were in Germany, but I will use this example for the end of that process. We left Germany after *believing God wanted us to stay there* and help build His Church there. That did not happen, and He led us to the state of Washington. Three nights in a row, God awakened my husband to a tall, red-haired preacher on television from Seattle, Washington. We could not understand why God was showing him this, until we went home to the United States for two weeks. Upon our return, we were told we had two weeks to get out of Germany and to get to our new duty assignment...in Washington. And sure enough, we joined the church my husband saw on television those three nights God spoke to Him through that situation. We didn't hear that audible voice; God revealed it through another avenue. He truly orders the steps of the righteous!

❖ The "still small voice" of Holy Spirit

"Then He said, "Go out, and stand on the mountain before the LORD." And behold, the LORD passed by, and a great and strong wind tore into the mountains and broke the rocks in pieces before the LORD, but the LORD was not in the wind; and after the wind an earthquake, but the LORD was not in the earthquake; and after the earthquake a fire, but the LORD was not in the fire; and after the fire a *still small voice*. So it was, when Elijah heard it, that he wrapped his face in his mantle and went out and stood in the entrance of the cave. Suddenly a voice came to him, and said, "What are you doing here, Elijah?""
1 Kings 19:11-13, emphasis

How often do we desire to hear God in the "outrageous" supernatural manifestations of the Spirit? Elijah was used to supernatural feats and awe inspiring victories; He could hear God clearly in those places. But what would happen when he was isolated, in a cold, dark cave? God came to Elijah in a different way, out of his comfort zone, to give the prophet instructions.

After leaving Germany and being in Seattle for four years, my husband was in Korea planning to return to Seattle where *we had planned* to retire from the military. I was at a conference at our church and there was a visiting pastor there from Colorado. I had heard of him through my daughter, as he preached at her Youth Conference, but I had never heard of him and never seen him preach before.

He was a very passionate preacher; he roared across the microphone and engaged the crowd as they shouted. I usually sat at the front, but this night, I was almost near the back, as I had served greeting the conference attendees that night. My head was hurting tremendously, as the noise was a little too much for me. Halfway through the service, I heard God say, "I am sending you to Colorado." What??? I *thought* we were retiring in Seattle? I began to weep right there in the service. My husband was on a fourteen hour

Holy Spirit

time difference, so I did not bother to call him. Well, as I got in my truck, I got a call from my beloved husband. He asked me if I was at the conference, and I explained to him that, indeed, I was. He told me that he normally was not able to live stream the services, because of the time difference, but this night, he could not sleep, and God told him to turn on the computer. As you can guess, he heard the same thing I heard, "You are going to Colorado." What??? I did not know until afterwards that this very pastor preaching this night was a pastor in Colorado and God was sending us to this man's church.

God has an uncanny way of speaking to His children and will go out of His way to be sure we are walking on the path of His perfect will to fulfill His plans for our lives. Open your hearts, and your ears, to receive Him in whatever way He chooses to speak to us. Let's look at several more scriptures revealing how God speaks to His people through the Voice of Holy Spirit:

"The Spirit of the LORD spoke through me; his word was on my tongue." 2 Samuel 23:2

"And while Peter was reflecting on the vision, the Spirit said to him, "Behold, three men are looking for you." Acts 10:19

"And while they were ministering to the Lord and fasting, the Holy Spirit said, "Set apart for Me Barnabas and Saul for the work to which I have called them." Acts 13:2

"And when they did not agree with one another, they began leaving after Paul had spoken one parting word, "The Holy Spirit rightly spoke through Isaiah the prophet to your fathers, saying, 'Go to this people and say, "You will keep on hearing, but will not understand." Acts 28:25-26

"And I heard a voice from heaven, saying, "Write, 'Blessed are the dead who die in the Lord from now on!'" "Yes," says the

Spirit," that they may rest from their labors, for their deeds follow with them." Revelation 14:13

God speaks to His people in many different ways, for many different reasons and through many different avenues. This reveals the extent to which He will go to get His heart to His people. He is not a God that is far from His Creation. He is very near, even within. His Holy Spirit dwells within His beloved and He is speaking...are we listening? No matter what you have gone through in your life, no matter what church you went to or church doctrine you were taught, no matter how you were hurt, even if it was done in the "name of religion," I am here to tell you that God wants to speak to you. He has magnificent plans for your life and desires to communicate with you. Open up your heart and receive Him today!

"Therefore, just as the Holy Spirit says, 'Today if you *hear His voice*, Do not harden your hearts as when they provoked Me, as in the day of trial in the wilderness," Hebrews 3:7-8, emphasis

---

John G. Lake

"The ministry of Christianity is the ministry of the Spirit. It is the Spirit of God that inhabits the words, that speaks to the spirit of another and reveals Christ in and through him."

"There is a mighty lot of difference between saying prayers and praying." ~John G. Lake

---

Chapter 14

He That Has an Ear to Hear

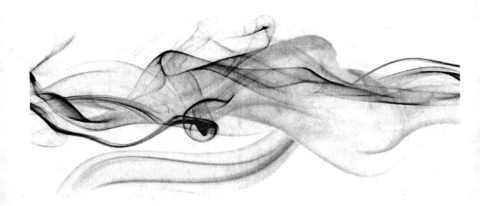

"He who has an ear, let him hear what the Spirit says to the churches. To him who overcomes, I will grant to eat of the tree of life, which is in the Paradise of God." Revelation 2:7

To hear the voice of God is only just the beginning. Wow! After all of this, getting to know the person, the purpose, the position, the power, the promise, and the partnership of Holy Spirit, learning how to develop an intimate relationship with Father God, and seeing how He operates through each of His assignments, you mean to tell me there's more? Yes, I am absolutely telling you that this is just scratching the surface of walking in the fullness of God.

There is much more God desires to do in and through His people and it is going to take complete surrender spiritually in faith and trust in His leading. This is another realm that not many Believers walk in, yet they criticize and contend with those that do. Understand that if there is no revelation, there can be no receiving. Many have not been taught these things, yet they are openly available in the Word of God for all that will receive. Others have, yet without the illumination Holy Spirit provides, they cannot break through to that next level of spiritual maturation. We are spiritual beings, and God speaks to us by and through His Spirit; the world and most Believers, cannot understand it.

"But God has revealed them to us through His Spirit. For the Spirit searches all things, yes, the deep things of God. For what man knows the things of a man except the spirit of the man which is in him? Even so no one knows the things of God except the Spirit of God. Now we have received, not the spirit of the world, but the Spirit who is from God, that we might know the things that have been freely given to us by God. These things we also speak, not in words which man's wisdom teaches but which the Holy Spirit teaches, comparing spiritual things with spiritual. But the natural man does not receive the things of the Spirit of God, for they are foolishness to him; nor can he know them, because they are spiritually discerned."
2 Corinthians 2:9-14

We must seek "higher ground" as we journey into the deep things of God. We cannot allow those that choose not to receive Holy Spirit to move us from our position in the Spirit. We should be so settled in our hearts, our minds and in our spirits that we are unmovable against the schemes of the enemy, even when he uses those in the Church to come up against us. But we have to deal with the basics. We cannot walk fully in the things of God and continue to house the presence of God, Holy Spirit, within if sin continues to have a stronghold over our lives. If we are in sin, we are separated from His presence. We must choose to humble ourselves and repent, and turn back to the Lord. The universal call since the fall of man, and even after our Lord's death, burial, resurrection and ascension, and until the day He cracks the sky and plants His feet on the Mount of Olives, is that of *repentance*. Many in the church today refuse to receive Holy Spirit, because they refuse to repent. They are living carnally and worldly. They believe they are 'once saved and always saved,' and see no need for repentance. This is a very dangerous belief.

Repentance is a key to the Kingdom that is rarely ever preached in today's church. Even if sin is touched upon, if we never preach on the need to repent, the heart of man is left open to go back to things it knows and is comfortable in. I believe we have all but lost respect and honor for the Lord and His Holy Spirit, because we refuse to live by the Word we say we were saved by. We have become hypocrites! The word *repentance* is defined as means to turn, the activity of reviewing one's actions and feeling contrition or regret for past wrongs. It generally involves a commitment to personal change and the resolve to live a more responsible and humane life. The Greek word for repentance is *metanoia* meaning repentance, a change of mind, or change in the inner man. When Holy Spirit convicts us through correction, whether it is by the Word, Himself, or another individual, we must humble ourselves and receive it, so that not only are we able to overcome the disobedience, but so that others will not feel comfortable in theirs. We must have a change of mind and completely turn away from it.

"He who has ears to hear, let him hear!" Matthew 13:9

Those that are comfortable in their sin choose not to hear the voice of God; some can no longer hear, because they are so stuck in the muck and mire of their sin. Many in the church today are in great bondage and God desires to set us free! His desire for us has not changed. He is Healer, Deliverer, Provider, Restorer and Redeemer. He wants to send a fresh wind of Holy Spirit through the lives of His people and through His Church. We have yet to see what the true Church of the Living God in the earth looks like, but it is coming!

"But as it is written: Eye has not seen, nor ear heard, Nor have entered into the heart of man the things which God has prepared for those who love Him." 1 Corinthians 2:19

The Hebrew word for repentance is *Teshuvah* meaning to return; it is a combination of turning away from evil and turning toward good. Many in today's church believe that repentance is merely asking God for forgiveness, but it is much more. We can ask Him all day to forgive us, but until we make the conscious choice to change our mind and literally turn away from the sin in our lives and turn toward Him and His Word, we will continue to practice a lifestyle of sin and be separated from His presence. *Teshuvah* is the Hebrew word assigned to the forty days preceding Yom Kippur, the Day of the Covering or Atonement. Originally, it only comprised the ten days between Rosh Hashanah and Yom Kippur (Days of Awe). But Jewish tradition extended this time of repentance so that all could come to the place of salvation. Every morning during *Teshuvah* the shofar will blow signifying, or warning everyone to "turn to God in repentance".

I traveled to California about a month ago and I knew this was going to be a turning point in my life. I met a precious man about ten years ago in Germany that God used to prophesy over my life. I have had several other people to prophesy over me, and all were accurate, but something was absolutely different about this prophet. Something totally shifted in my life as he prophesied these simple, yet profound words into my spirit, "God is calling you as a *conduit* to His people." I somewhat had an idea of what God was saying, as many words were lining up and opening up to me, but I had no idea of the extent of what this prophecy meant in my life. Fast forward ten years, and here I am meeting this precious prophet face to face once again. I believe greatly in *kairos* moments, God's divinely orchestrated seasons for each of us.

216

As I was landing in California, I heard the Spirit of the Lord say, "A sound will be released from this place; a shofar will blow in the Spirit." The entire weekend was truly a touch from Heaven. God met us each day and each night and Holy Spirit dwelt strongly among us. The Word, the Worship, the healings, deliverance, prophecy and salvation sprung up in every service. It wasn't a *strange* or *out of control* display of supernatural occurrences, but it flowed, all in order, and God was glorified. I can honestly say after over thirty years of being saved and twenty walking in Christ, this was the absolute *first* time I had experienced the fullness of God in a corporate setting. I have been in mega churches with over ten thousand people, and have not witnessed such oneness in the Spirit in *every* aspect of the service.

On that Saturday night, the man of God had a sermon, as well as several people that were going to minister and share testimonies, but the Spirit of God had another plan. Worship went to a different level each time we met in this place, from Friday night, Saturday morning and now to the night service...it was so thick with His presence that we could not seem to come out of it? The man of God was led right into a prophetic display of healing, deliverance and activation. Gifts of tongues and interpretation sprung up, words of wisdom and knowledge, prophetic declarations, bodies healed right there in the service, people walking down the aisle to the altar that had not walked in years, and so much more. I could barely stand in this atmosphere. I just wept and wept, praying and singing in the Spirit and giving God glory.

Near the end of the service, the man of God called my name and asked me to come to the altar. The atmosphere was so sparked with excitement and expectation at what God had done and what we were sure He would continue to do in our midst. As I stood face to face with the prophet that had prophesied into my life ten years earlier, he began to reveal another level, another realm, God was calling me to in being His voice in the earth realm. I will not share the prophecy here, as it is to be covered and only heard by

Holy Spirit

those that were in that meeting in California. He activated the calling on my life this night, as only he could; it was a culmination of ten years of walking through the darkest seasons of my life in the wilderness, as well as the most beautiful seasons of my life hearing from the voice of the Lord. I was in my process, in preparation, for this very moment in time.

A word was released out of my spirit and it was the simple, yet absolutely pertinent message of *repentance*. The once electrified mood of the meeting turned to a silent room that was met with the weeping of the Lord for humanity. For me, it was a travail in my spirit that I had not ever witnessed. I have interceded greatly over the years for repentance, but this was notably different. God challenged us this night in ways unimaginable. The signs, wonders and miracles are great, and yes, a part of God revealing His love for us, but there was a deeper truth He needed for us to hear; a deeper truth that He is calling the Church to receive. I had seventy and eighty year old men and women coming up to me with tears in their eyes completely broken before the Lord. I am sure some may not have received, as in any setting, but something happened that night that not only transformed hearts, but it also infuriated our adversary, Satan. The message of repentance is probably the greatest message he has tried and continues to try and eradicate from the lives of God's people and the Church. He understands the magnitude of authentic, heartfelt repentance, and therefore launches an all out assault against anyone that surrenders to God in such a way. And he will try to destroy anyone that speaks out boldly concerning repentance. It is not some great, new revelation; it has been the cry of the ages.

I was unaware, until studying for this chapter that the *shofar* was a symbol used as a call of repentance. On Rosh Hashanah, the first of the *Ten Days of Repentance*, the Jews awaken from spiritual slumber. The *shofar* is like an alarm that calls God's people to examine their deeds and correct their ways, as they return to Him. I believe the Word I heard from Holy Spirit as I landed in California

218

was not just a Word for this meeting, but a universal "blowing of the shofar" to the nations of the world. God is calling us to awaken from our sleep, to arise and become; the world is eagerly awaiting the manifestation of the sons of God. The Kingdom of God is at hand.

Let's look at the multi-generational call of repentance from the Beginning to the End. God's plan hasn't changed, and neither has His timeless Word.

The Call of Repentance from the Prophets/Apostles

❖ FROM THE PROPHET ISAIAH

"This is what the Sovereign LORD, the Holy One of Israel, says: "In repentance and rest is your salvation, in quietness and trust is your strength, but you would have none of it." Isaiah 30:15

❖ FROM THE PROPHET JEREMIAH

"Go and proclaim these words toward the north, and say: 'Return, backsliding Israel,' says the Lord; 'I will not cause My anger to fall on you. For I am merciful,' says the Lord; 'I will not remain angry forever. Only acknowledge your iniquity, That you have transgressed against the Lord your God, And have scattered your charms to alien deities under every green tree, And you have not obeyed My voice,' says the Lord. "Return, O backsliding children," says the Lord; "for I am married to you. I will take you, one from a city and two from a family, and I will bring you to Zion. And I will give you shepherds according to My heart, who will feed you with knowledge and understanding." (Jeremiah 3:12-15)

❖ FROM THE PROPHET JOEL

"Blow the shofar in Zion (Remember, the shofar is blown everyday during the time of and sound an alarm in My holy mountain...Now

219

therefore, says the Lord, Turn to Me with all your heart, with fasting, weeping, and with mourning...Return to the Lord, your God..." (Joel 2:1 and 12-13, Torah)

❖ FROM THE PROPHET HOSEA

"Come, and let us return to the Lord; For He has torn, but He will heal us; He has stricken, but He will bind us up." (Hosea 6:1)

❖ FROM THE PROPHET EZEKIEL

"Therefore say to the house of Israel, 'Thus says the Lord God: "Repent, turn away from your idols, and turn your faces away from all your abominations." (Ezekiel 14:6)

❖ FROM THE PROPHET ZECHARIAH

"Therefore say to them, 'Thus says the Lord of hosts: "Return to Me," says the Lord of hosts, "and I will return to you," says the Lord of hosts. "Do not be like your fathers, to whom the former prophets preached, saying, 'Thus says the Lord of hosts: "Turn now from your evil ways and your evil deeds."' But they did not hear nor heed Me," says the Lord." (Zechariah 1:3-4)

❖ FROM THE PROPHET JOHN, THE BAPTIST

"...Repent, for the kingdom of heaven is at hand." (Matthew 3:2)

"Therefore bear fruits worthy of repentance, and do not begin to say to yourselves, 'We have Abraham as our father.' For I say to you that God is able to raise up children to Abraham from these stones. And even now the ax is laid to the root of the trees. Therefore every tree which does not bear good fruit is cut down and thrown into the fire." (Luke 3:8-9)

❖ FROM THE APOSTLE PETER

"Repent therefore and be converted, that your sins may be blotted out, so that times of refreshing may come from the presence of the Lord." (Acts 3:19)

"The Lord is not slack concerning His promise, as some count slackness, but is longsuffering toward us, not willing that any should perish but that all should come to repentance." 2 Peter 3:9

❖ FROM THE APOSTLE PAUL

"Therefore, King Agrippa, I was not disobedient to the heavenly vision, but declared first to those in Damascus and in Jerusalem, and throughout all the region of Judea, and then to the Gentiles, that they should repent, turn to God, and do works befitting repentance." Acts 26:19-20

"But because of your stubbornness and your unrepentant heart, you are storing up wrath against yourself for the day of God's wrath, when his righteous judgment will be revealed." Romans 2:5

❖ FROM JESUS CHRIST

"From that time Jesus began to preach, saying, "Repent, for the kingdom of heaven is at hand." (Matthew 4:17)

"I have not come to call the righteous but sinners to repentance." (Luke 5:32)

"The men of Nineveh will rise up at the judgment with this generation and condemn it, for they repented at the preaching of Jonah, and behold, something greater than Jonah is here." (Matthew 12:41)

"Unless you repent, you will all likewise perish." (Luke 13:3, 5)

From the moment Jesus stepped into His earthly ministry, the first message He preached was, "Repent…" Those before Him called for repentance and those after Him called for repentance. If this is not the focal message of the Church today, then we are not preaching the Gospel of Jesus Christ, or the message of the Kingdom. The Word has not *emerged*, or *evolved*; His Word is forever settled in Heaven and it is the same yesterday, today and forevermore. Most seem to think we are in an entirely new dispensation than that of the early disciples, the early Church, but this is absolutely false. From the time Jesus ascended to glory and the Holy Spirit was poured out upon His followers, the Church age began and will not end, until He comes again. The Book of Revelation, from the beginning, stresses the underlying theme of repentance and having an *ear to hear* what the Spirit of God is speaking.

"The Revelation of Jesus Christ, which God gave Him to show His servants-things which must shortly take place. And He sent and signified it by His angel to His servant John, who bore witness to the Word of God, and to the testimony of Jesus Christ, to all things that he saw. Blessed is he who reads and those who *hear* the words of this prophecy, and keep those things that are written in it; for the time is near." Revelation 1:1-3

Many that believe in the working of Holy Spirit within the lives of those that follow Jesus Christ, call Him the "inner witness," "the knower," "the unction," or the "ear of our spirit". The inner workings of Holy Spirit are absolutely profound. He is the initiator of humility, brokenness, reverence, surrender, submission, sacrifice, and yes, repentance. The *hearing* most understand is that of the previous keys we covered: the Word, Prayer, Worship, etc., but the *ear of our spirits* is the apex of our spiritual maturation; complete oneness and agreement with our Father, hearing and moving, flowing in unity with Heaven's wind…*Holy Spirit.*

He That Has an Ear to Hear

The message of *hearing* to the 7 Churches:

- CHURCH AT EPHESUS

"Nevertheless I have this against you, that you have left your first love. Remember therefore from where you have fallen; repent and do the first works, or else I will come to you quickly and remove your lampstand from its place—unless you repent. But this you have, that you hate the deeds of the Nicolaitans, which I also hate." Revelation 2:4-6

"He who has an ear, let him hear what the Spirit says to the churches. To him who overcomes I will give to eat from the tree of life, which is in the midst of the Paradise of God."'

- CHURCH AT SMYRNA

"Do not fear any of those things which you are about to suffer. Indeed, the devil is about to throw some of you into prison, that you may be tested, and you will have tribulation ten days. Be faithful until death, and I will give you the crown of life." Revelation 2:10-11

"He who has an ear, let him hear what the Spirit says to the churches. He who overcomes shall not be hurt by the second death."'

- CHURCH OF PERGAMOS

"But I have a few things against you, because you have there those who hold the doctrine of Balaam, who taught Balak to put a stumbling block before the children of Israel, to eat things sacrificed to idols, and to commit sexual immorality. Thus you also have those who hold the doctrine of the Nicolaitans, which thing I hate. Repent, or else I will come to you quickly and will fight against them with the sword of My mouth." Revelation 2:14-16

"He who has an ear, let him hear what the Spirit says to the churches. To him who overcomes I will give some of the hidden manna to eat. And I will give him a white stone, and on the stone a new name written which no one knows except him who receives it.'"

• CHURCH OF THYATIRA

"Nevertheless I have a few things against you, because you allow that woman Jezebel, who calls herself a prophetess, to teach and seduce My servants to commit sexual immorality and eat things sacrificed to idols. And I gave her time to repent of her sexual immorality, and she did not repent." Revelation 2:20-21

"But hold fast what you have till I come. And he who overcomes, and keeps My works until the end, to him I will give power over the nations— 'He shall rule them with a rod of iron; They shall be dashed to pieces like the potter's vessels'—as I also have received from My Father; and I will give him the morning star."

"He who has an ear, let him hear what the Spirit says to the churches.'"

• CHURCH OF SARDIS

"I know your works, that you have a name that you are alive, but you are dead. Be watchful, and strengthen the things which remain, that are ready to die, for I have not found your works perfect before God. Remember therefore how you have received and heard; hold fast and repent. Therefore if you will not watch, I will come upon you as a thief, and you will not know what hour I will come upon you. You have a few names even in Sardis who have not defiled their garments; and they shall walk with Me in white, for they are worthy." Revelation 3:1b-4

"He who overcomes shall be clothed in white garments, and I will not blot out his name from the Book of Life; but I will confess his name before My Father and before His angels."

"He who has an ear, let him hear what the Spirit says to the churches."

- ### CHURCH OF PHILADELPHIA

"These things says He who is holy, He who is true, "He who has the key of David, He who opens and no one shuts, and shuts and no one opens": "I know your works. See, I have set before you an open door, and no one can shut it; for you have a little strength, have kept My word, and have not denied My name. Indeed I will make those of the synagogue of Satan, who say they are Jews and are not, but lie—indeed I will make them come and worship before your feet, and to know that I have loved you. Because you have kept My command to persevere, I also will keep you from the hour of trial which shall come upon the whole world, to test those who dwell on the earth. Behold, I am coming quickly! Hold fast what you have, that no one may take your crown." Revelation 3:7b-11

"He who overcomes, I will make him a pillar in the temple of My God, and he shall go out no more. I will write on him the name of My God and the name of the city of My God, the New Jerusalem, which comes down out of heaven from My God. And I will write on him My new name."

"He who has an ear, let him hear what the Spirit says to the churches."

- ### CHURCH OF LAODICEA

"These things says the Amen, the Faithful and True Witness, the Beginning of the creation of God: "I know your works, that you are neither cold nor hot. I could wish you were cold or hot. So then, because you are lukewarm, and neither cold nor hot, I will vomit you out of My mouth. Because you say, 'I am rich, have become wealthy, and have need of nothing'—and do not know that you are wretched, miserable, poor, blind, and naked—I counsel you to buy from Me gold refined in the fire, that you may be rich; and white garments, that you may be clothed, that the shame of your nakedness may not be revealed; and anoint your eyes with eye salve, that you may see. As many as I love, I rebuke and chasten. Therefore be zealous and repent. Behold, I stand at the door and knock. If anyone *hears My voice* and opens the door, I will come in to him and dine with him, and he with Me." Revelation 3:14b-20

"To him who overcomes I will grant to sit with Me on My throne, as I also overcame and sat down with My Father on His throne."

"He who has an ear, let him hear what the Spirit says to the churches."

We must earnestly heed the warnings of these scriptures. Please don't be naïve in thinking this was a mere warning to the early church; this message is for the universal Church throughout the generations. Read thoroughly and open the ears of your spirit. Do you see yourself in any of these passages? If Holy Spirit touches you and points out anything, be quick to hear and repent and receive His prophetic Promise over your life. He is able to refine us, reform us, renew us, restore us, revive us, redeem us and reconcile us to the Father as we submit to the Word and to the leading of His Spirit...*Holy Spirit.*

The true Church of the Living God, His *Ekklesia*, will hear His voice, are now hearing His voice, and completely surrendering their lives to Him in broken repentance. The *Ekklesia* are the "called out ones". Do you have an *ear to hear*?

"After these things I looked, and behold, a door standing open in heaven. And the first *voice which I heard* was like a trumpet speaking with me, saying, "Come up here, and I will show you things which must take place after this. Immediately I was in the Spirit; and behold, a throne set in heaven, and One sat on the throne." Revelation 4:1-2, emphasis

God has given us His precious Holy Spirit who teaches us how to hear His voice, but also trains us to have *ears to hear* in ways only He is able. Open your heart, open your ears and open your spirit to hear what the Spirit of the Lord is saying to you. He has much He desires to share...receive *Holy Spirit* today!

Myles Monroe

"The nature of this relationship between the unseen world of the Kingdom government and the seen world of the physical earth underscores the incalculable value of the One who makes the connection between these two realms possible...the Holy Spirit."

"Under the guidance and enabling of the Holy Spirit, we are the Kingdom's representative..." ~Myles Monroe

Epilogue

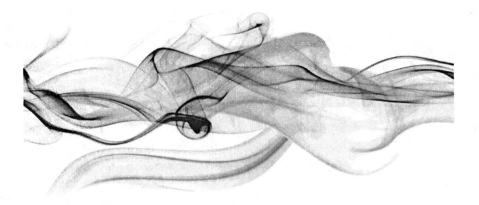

"The Spirit of the Lord God is upon Me; because the Lord hath anointed Me to preach good tidings unto the meek; He hath sent me to bind up the brokenhearted, to proclaim liberty to the captives, and the opening of the prison to them that are bound."

Isaiah 61: 1-3

This book is not for everyone; it is for those that choose to hear what the Spirit of God is saying and sense His convicting presence, unction, to go higher. This book is for those that hunger and thirst after righteousness and desire to go to deeper levels in God. This book is for those that have the heart of God and a heart for building His Kingdom in the earth realm. A people are rising that are breaking the religious chains of oppression, getting back to the foundational truths of the Word of God, demanding purity and holiness in Worship and Prayer, reclaiming the "childlike" faith that leads to the Kingdom, and walking in power, authority and dominion in this dark world, shifting societal norms and fighting for the less fortunate all over the world. This outpouring and awakening that is happening all over the world is not a move of man, but literally, the hand of God, through *Holy Spirit!*

To understand who Holy Spirit is and what His role is in our lives, as well as the Body of Christ, is the most precious gift in this earth. How many across the world have no idea the depths of His assignment? How many know, yet refuse to teach or speak concerning Him? Why in the world would those that have the truth not want to share it with the world? Or more importantly, the Church? I spoke in the first couple of chapters about a spirit in operation that has desires to stifle and even eradicate the voice of God in the earth realm. This spirit has tried to uproot every trace of God in society and is turning this world upside down with deception and darkness. This is the anti-Christ spirit and it is the spirit behind every other demonic spirit in operation today. When people's eyes and ears are opened, through the voice and leading of Holy Spirit, these spirits are exposed and God's people become free. The only way to defeat this spirit is to walk in the absolute fullness of God, Christ likeness, in the earth realm. A people that have allowed the Word of God to become *flesh* within them, living breathing epistles, revealed to the world as the sons of God Almighty. The anti-Christ spirit can only dwell in a people that don't know their true identity in Christ, and Holy Spirit is a major factor in God revealing to His people His true intent for their lives.

Once we have reconnected with God's original intent for mankind and step back into the "Garden" (the place of dominion) we will literally become One with Father God, complete union with our Creator. He promises to those of us that overcome, He will grant to eat of the tree of life, which is in the Paradise of God. My brothers and sisters, this is not our home. We are just passing through this life on assignment. We have much work to do for the

Kingdom of God. We are in this world, but not of this world. We can live in a higher spiritual state and commune with Father God in ways unimaginable to the natural world. Heaven and Earth meet through the conduit of the precious presence of God... *Holy Spirit*. We have the power of the Holy One dwelling within and He is ready and willing to show you and speak to you things you would never imagine possible with Father God. This world has nothing to offer you, but an eternal life of darkness and despair. Receive your freedom today and the chains of oppression will fall off of you. The Light of His Word will pierce through the darkness that has you bound and the gates of those prison doors that have kept you locked in depression and destruction for years will swing wide open! Holy Spirit is here to help you; you are not alone.

He works alongside Father and Son, bringing us into His fullness, complete union, to rule and reign with Him, not only in heavenly places, but we have the power and authority to help bring Heaven's purposes to the earth realm with the aid of Holy Spirit. We were created for dominion! Our beloved Holy Spirit, the *Ruach Ha Ko'desh*, the spirit of holiness, the breath of the Holy One, within has the power to transform our entire lives for the glory of Father God. His abiding manifest presence dwells within those that are His; heaven and earth becoming one.

Today, you can receive the *indwelling* and *infilling* power of God through Holy Spirit. Simply declare this prayer from your heart:

"Father, Your Word says if I ask for Holy Spirit, you will give Him to me. I may have resisted His promptings in my life and even grieved Him, through fear or even disobedience. I repent of my sins and turn away from them and look to You. Wash me and cleanse me and make me new. I believe there is more that You desire to show me and more that you want to do through my life for Your Kingdom. I surrender and submit my life to You. My life is no longer my own. This is not my home; I am merely on assignment. I will purpose to let Holy Spirit lead me, instruct me, help me, teach me, comfort me, counsel me, correct me, intercede through me and reveal to me all that needs to be imparted into my life, so that it may glorify You. I am Your's Lord!"

"Without the Holy Spirit, Christianity is reduced to 'religion'."
~Reinhard Bonnke

God is building His Ekklesia, His army; the Army of the Lord is rising and it will not be according to the flesh, but *BY HIS SPIRIT!* What we are witnessing before our very eyes all over the world cannot be addressed by mere words; it must be strategically confronted *in, by, from* and *through* the spiritual realm, Holy Spirit within the lives of born-again Believers in Christ Jesus. We may be in this world, but we are not *of* this world. God is calling His people higher and those that have ears to hear *are hearing* and mobilizing and moving out in all power, authority and dominion by the leading of *Holy Spirit.* They look, sound, talk and walk like the early church, they will be ridiculed, mocked and persecuted by not only the world, but also by the organized church. They are *disrupters*, as Jesus and His disciples were and are completely sold out and surrendered to the Gospel. They have counted all the costs and have said, "YES! I WILL GO! SEND ME!" These are *they* that will turn this world upside down for Jesus Christ! What a time to be living in!

About the Author

Deborah G. Hunter is a wife, mother, author, inspirational speaker, and CEO & Publisher of Hunter Heart Publishing. She has written four books of her own, Breaking the Eve Mentality, Raising Your Prophet, and The Call of Intercession and her new bestseller The Wilderness. Deborah travels nationally & internationally on her mission to "Offer God's Heart to a Dying World" through the inspired gift of writing, personal testimony, and through the gifts God has placed in her. She serves as an avid philanthropist through her charity, *Stir Up the Gift*, dedicated to providing support for the needy around the world, including the country of Japan after the wake of the 2011 Earthquake/Tsunami that ravaged this country.

Deborah has been a born-again believer since the age of twelve and has been on her pathway to destiny ever since. She was ordained as a Minister in Prophetic Gifting on July 7, 2007 in Kitzingen, Germany from International Gospel Church. She received her Bachelor's of Arts Degree in Biblical Studies/Theology from Minnesota Graduate School of Theology.

Deborah is married to Chris Hunter, Jr., radio personality and CEO of Hunter Entertainment Network, a conglomerate of Christian media outlets, including record label, movie, book, and music production companies. They share in the raising of their three children together, Jade, Elijah, and Ja'el, and are the father and step-mother of three, along with three beautiful grandchildren. They reside in the beautiful mountains of Colorado.

Bibliography

[i] *Who is the Holy Spirit in Islam?* King Hassan II, the Alaouite Dynasty. http://www.safne.com/azali11.htm

[ii] http://www.theopedia.com/regeneration

[iii] Morris, Charles. *The Four Positions of Holy Spirit.* (Westbow Press, A Division of Thomas Nelson & Zondervan, Nashville, TN). Published 2014.

[iv] Tozer, A.W. *The Knowledge of the Holy.* (New York: Harper and Row), p. 73

[v] Charisma Magazine. Article. Grady, J. Lee. *6 Things That Block the Holy Spirit's Power.* May 20, 2015.

[vi] Ausburger, Myron, S. *Quench Not the Spirit.* (Herald Press; Rev. edition (1975)

[vii] *Types of Intimacy.* http://www.counseling.ufl.edu/cwc/types-of-intimacy.aspx. University of Florida Counseling & Wellness Center, Gaines-ville, FL.

[viii] Stedman, Ray C. *Authentic Christianity.* (Discovery House Publishers, Grand Rapids, Michigan. Published 1996.

[ix] Hunter, Deborah G. *The Wilderness.* (Hunter Heart Publishing, Colorado Springs, Colorado. Published 2014

[x] Bevere, John. *Good or God? Why Good Without God Isn't Good Enough.* (Messenger International, Palmer Lake, Colorado. Published 2015

[xi] Worship Leader magazine- http://worshipleader.com/leadership/hearing-god-speak/. Published 2014.

PRAYER FOR SALVATION

"God, I come to You in the Name of Jesus. I ask You to come into my life. I confess with my mouth that Jesus is my Lord and I believe in my heart that You have raised Him from the dead. I turn my back on sin and I commit to follow You for the rest of my life. I thank You, Father, for saving me!"

If you have prayed this prayer for the first time, we would love to hear from you. You can email us at:

publisher@hunterheartpublishing.com

or you can visit our webpage at:

www.hunterheartpublishing.com

Facebook:

Hunter Heart Publishing/Hunter Entertainment Network

...and submit a prayer request.

We would love to pray with you and help you to find a local church to get connected to, so you can grow in the Lord.

OTHER BOOKS BY
DEBORAH G. HUNTER
AVAILABLE NOW AT
WWW.HUNTERHEARTPUBLISHING.COM
AMAZON.COM, BARNES & NOBLE
AND ALL MAJOR CHRISTIAN BOOKSTORES
AND OUTLETS WORLDWIDE!

website: www.hunterheartpublishing.com
Facebook: Deborah G. Hunter
Twitter: @hunterheartpub
YouTube: Hunter Heart Publishing

OTHER BOOKS BY
DEBORAH G. HUNTER
COMING SOON!

THE WILDERNESS SERIES

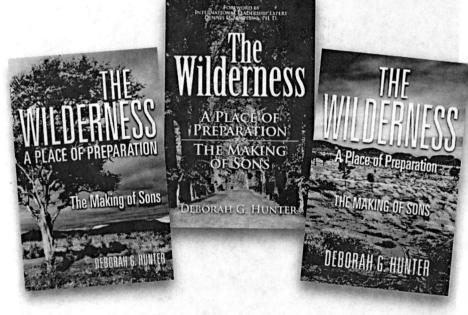

website: www.hunterheartpublishing.com
Facebook: Deborah G. Hunter
Twitter: @hunterheartpub
YouTube: Hunter Heart Publishing

OTHER BOOKS BY
DEBORAH G. HUNTER
COMING SOON!

website: www.hunterheartpublishing.com
Facebook: Deborah G. Hunter
Twitter: @hunterheartpub
YouTube: Hunter Heart Publishing

Wed. 3-21-18

James 2:19 demons believe - and tremble

Thur. april 5-18

Excepted Lord 1978 - Baptized Holy Spirit
Moved to Calif 1982
Moved to Covelo, CA. 1992
Moved to Sothern Calif. with Beth 2002
Moved to Phils Shandon, CA. 2010
Ken Passed May 1 2012
Ina Jane april 15-2016
Moved with Beth Fall 2016
Back in Calif.
From 1978 to 2018 = 40 yrs.
   Same amount of theme the
   Isrealites were in the desert
   I am trusting Jesus in all
   areas of my life

9 781937 741518